TEXT AND INTERPRETATION

REVELATION

A Practical Commentary

L. van Hartingsveld

Translated by John Vriend

GRAND RAPIDS, MICHIGAN
WILLIAM B. EERDMANS PUBLISHING COMPANY

Translated from the Dutch edition *Openbaring: Een praktische bijbelverklaring*, part of the Tekst en Toelichting series. © Uitgeversmaatschappij J. H. Kok—Kampen, 1984.

Library of Congress Cataloging-in-Publication Data

Hartingsveld, L. van, 1916-
  Revelation.

  (Text and interpretation)
  Translation of: Openbaring.
  1.Bible. N.T. Revelation—Commentaries. I. Bible.
N.T. Revelation. English. Revised Standard. 1985.
II. Title. III. Series.
BS2825.3.H345 1985   228'.077   85-16075

ISBN 0-8028-0100-5 (pbk.)

CONTENTS

TRANSLATOR'S PREFACE

In translating this volume from the Dutch original, I have consistently tried to make it both readable and readily useful, for the pastor as well as for the layperson.

Bible quotations are from the Revised Standard Version, except where the author's own translation was closer in letter and spirit to another version. In those cases, I followed the appropriate version—New International, New English, or occasionally other versions—and indicated this in the text. When for some reason the translation was not intelligible without additional explanation, I have supplied a footnote.

It is my earnest wish that users of this commentary may derive as much pleasure and instruction from reading it as I did in translating it.

—JOHN VRIEND

INTRODUCTION

If there is any Bible book that needs explanation it must be the Revelation of John. The number of commentaries on it is legion.

The common idea that this is Scripture that predicts the great events of all future ages has been the cause of many misunderstandings. Over and over the book was read as though John were personally acquainted with Luther, the pope, Napoleon, Hitler, and Churchill, and knew about the French Revolution, the inoculation of cattle, and the theory of evolution. Gog and Magog (Rev. 20:8) stood for communism; and Meshech and Tubal (Ezek. 38:2) were read as Moscow and Tobolsk. But such quasi profundity simply is not a good key. The first order of business is to listen attentively to what the book says. Then follows the question about a possible application.

I. PURPOSE

The Revelation of John transfers us to the Roman empire under the rule of Emperor Domitian (A.D. 81-96). John exhorts Christians to remain faithful and comforts the church with the victory of God and the Lamb. Some believers have already been martyred, one of whom Antipas, is mentioned by name (Rev. 2:13). John sees and hears the souls under the altar, who cry out for vengeance (6:9-10); he sees the souls of those who have been beheaded (20:4). The blood of saints and prophets has been shed (16:6). The woman sitting on the beast is drunk with the blood of the martyrs (17:6). The emperor had himself venerated as a god and anyone not cooperating had to fear the worst. But mighty Rome is sure to perish; God and his Anointed have the last word.

II. AUTHOR

There has been much discussion on the question of whether the author of the Revelation of John is the person who wrote the Gospel and the Epistles of John. We shall not deal with that question; even without knowing who composed Revelation it is very well possible to explain the book. (The issue is the same with the Letter to the Hebrews: we simply do not know who the author is. But that does not hinder us from reading and understanding that letter.)

From Revelation itself one can infer the following data concerning the author:

1. He is on the island of Patmos on account of the Word of God and the testimony of Jesus (1:9); it is generally believed he is there as an exile.
2. As appears from the seven letters to the churches in the Roman province of Asia (chapters 2 and 3), he has detailed knowledge of local circumstances.
3. He knows the history of the Roman emperors and is at home in the world of his day.
4. Like any other good "scribe," he is familiar with the Old Testament; his diction and style are so deeply stamped by this that his Greek can sometimes be understood only after being translated back into Hebrew.
5. He was a man of authority; if otherwise, the solemn assurance "I John am he who heard and saw these things" (22:8) makes no sense.

III. REVELATION

John is one of the servants to whom God showed what must shortly take place (1:1). To him was given a glimpse into the unknown future. He expressed what he saw in a form we call "apocalyptic." An Old Testament example of this type of literature can be found in the Book of Daniel (Dan. 7–12). Other examples from the Old Testament that come to mind are Isaiah 24–27; Ezekiel 38 and 39; Joel 2:28–3:21; and Zechariah 1–6, 9–14. It is not an accident, therefore, that John often makes his appeal to these parts of Scripture. We shall not consider extrabiblical apocalyptic because it is not easily available or accessible to the average church member.

The revelation relates to "the mystery of God" (10:7); that is, to God's plan for this world. When the seventh angel blows the trumpet, that plan will be realized without delay (10:7). What that means can be discovered from the songs of praise that follow the last trumpet: the establishment of the kingship of God and his Anointed on earth; the pouring out of his wrath upon rebellious nations; the resurrection of the dead; judgment, punishment, and reward (11:15-19). This, then, sums up the things that will be worked out in greater detail in chapters 12–22.

That is the great mystery; in addition, there are also smaller mysteries. Some can be easily guessed. For example, Babylon is Rome, capital of the empire (17:5, 18). Some mysteries are explained, such as the seven stars and the seven lampstands (1:20). Others, such as the number 666 (13:18) and the beast that "was and is not and is to come" (17:8-11), are a challenge to the decoders. The Hebrew serves well as a code-language. In Hebrew, the angel of the underworld is called "Abaddon"; knowing the Greek name, "Apollyon," which means Destroyer, helps to solve the riddle (9:11). The case is different, however, with the Hebrew word *Armageddon* (16:16), which is not translated, presumably because the copyists no longer knew its meaning.

The smaller mysteries call for "wisdom" and intelligence (13:18; 17:9). In the face of the great mystery of God (10:7), however, all human wisdom is inadequate. It requires revelation.

IV. SACRED NUMBERS

We cannot calculate the day of Christ's return. Jesus comes as a thief in the night (3:3; 16:15). Still, a lot of figuring takes place in Revelation. But that is done with numbers having a symbolic value. For instance, the number seven symbolizes totality. This symbolism is rooted in the image of the world that prevailed at that time. The earth was pictured as a flat disc floating like a cork on the ocean. Above the earth the vault of heaven was fixed. That gives us the familiar three-story world: heaven, earth, underworld (5:3, 13). The earth has four corners (Ezek. 7:2; Rev. 7:1; 20:8), which are the four points of the compass: North, South, East, and West (Jer. 49:36; Ezek. 37:9; Zech. 6:5; Dan. 7:2; Matt. 24:31; Mark 13:27;

Rev. 7:1). Add the three to the four, and you have seven. So seven is the entire universe, everything, the whole of existence, the totality.

That is the background in terms of which John so often works with the numbers three, four, and seven. The eagle cries "woe" three times (8:13). Three foul spirits issue from the mouths of the trio consisting of the dragon, the beast, and the false prophet (16:13). Around the throne stand four living creatures (4:6). Four angels hold back the storms (7:1). The scroll is sealed with seven seals (5:1). Seven trumpets are sounded (8:2). Angels pour out the seven bowls of wrath (16:1). John writes letters to seven churches (chaps. 2 and 3).

Not only can we add the numbers three and four; we can also multiply them, which yields twelve. The New Jerusalem has a wall with twelve gates with the names of the twelve tribes of Israel inscribed on them (21:12). The wall itself rests on twelve foundations on which the names of the twelve apostles are written (21:14).

The addition of twelve plus twelve, and the multiplication of twelve times twelve, also produces sacred numbers. Twenty-four elders are seated on twenty-four thrones (4:4). The wall is 144 cubits high (21:17). The number of the sealed is also 144 (7:4).

Similarly sacred is half of seven. The woman in the wilderness is nourished a time, times, and half a time (12:14). This determination of time is taken from Daniel. In June 168 B.C., the temple of Jerusalem was desecrated, because a pig was sacrificed on the altar. That happened three and a half years after the high priest Onias had been deposed. Daniel prophesied that the tyranny of Antiochus Epiphanes IV would also last three and a half years—a prediction that turned out to be very close, as the temple was rededicated in December 165 B.C. One time, two times, and half a time, then, equals three and a half years, which is forty-two months (11:2), or 1,260 days (11:3; 12:6); this indicates the period of Messianic woes that precedes the coming of the kingdom of God.

V. VISIONS

The revelation comes through visions. The construction materials for these visions are provided by the Old Testament, astrology, history, and the actual situation. The exposition will show this in detail, so we will offer only a couple of examples here. The beast that rises from the sea is unthinkable apart from the four beasts of Daniel 7. The story of the woman and the dragon is told by the stars (Rev. 12). One can understand what is meant by the woman on the scarlet beast (Rev. 17) only if one knows the history of the Roman emperors. The letters to the seven churches allude to concrete incidents that took place in those churches.

Those who adhere to the recapitulation theory believe that all the visions related to the same subject, and that there is no real progression in the book. The phrase "after this I saw" (4:1; 7:1; 7:9; 15:5; 18:1) refers only to the order of the visions and not to the chronological progression of the expected events. It seems to me, however, that this theory cannot be maintained. There is, in fact, clear evidence of a climax in the book. When the fourth seal is broken, a quarter of the people die (6:8). The catastrophes that follow the sounding of the six trumpets strike the third part of heaven, sea, and earth and the third part of the human population (chaps. 8 and 9). The seven bowls of the wrath of God are poured out upon all (chap. 16). Thus, the judgment becomes heavier each time. The martyrs cry out for vengeance. But God will avenge their blood only when the number of those who were to be killed would be complete (6:11). The dead who die in the Lord are pronounced blessed (14:13). Why? Because they were spared the worst, which is yet to come. Look at the example of war. First there is mention of war on a limited scale (6:1-8); next there is the war of the beast against Christians (13:7); finally there is a war of the entire world against Christianity (16:14). History occurs in stages and every stage shows an intensification of punishment and opposition. The separate judgments culminate in the final judgment (20:11-15).

VI. COMPOSITION

John was instructed to record what he had seen, what is, and what is to take place hereafter (1:19). He strictly followed this instruction. First, he tells the story of the way he was called (1:9-20). Second, his letters lay bare the actual situations of the churches (chaps. 2 and 3). Finally, three quarters of the book contain the revelation of what must soon take place

(4:1–22:5). He begins the whole book with a prologue (1:1-8) and ends with an epilogue (22:6-21).

Prologue and epilogue correspond. Revelation begins with a salutation (1:4-5) and ends with a benediction (22:21). The central theme of both is the return of Christ (1:7; 22:7, 12, 20). This surfaces again in the seven letters (chaps 2 and 3) but occurs only twice in the section dealing with what still has to take place (14:14; 16:15). Both at the beginning and at the end of the book we are told that the time is near (1:3; 22:10). Christ, or God, respectively, sends his angel to make known to his servants what is about to take place (1:1; 22:6). In the prologue God is the Alpha and the Omega (1:8), while Christ is described similarly in the epilogue (22:13). And as the final parallel we must refer to the blessing pronounced on those who carefully keep the prophetic words of Revelation (1:3; 22:13).

The main section (4:1–22:5) follows a scheme that is repeatedly interrupted. Seven seals. Seven trumpets. Seven bowls. When the seventh seal is broken one expects the end of history. But instead seven angels appear, who will blow the trumpets (8:1). Not even the last trumpet ushers in the consummation (11:15) but it is followed by seven angels with bowls filled with the wrath of God (15:1). When the last bowl is emptied the verdict on Babylon (Rome) is carried out (17:1–19:10); the beast, the false prophet, and the dragon are seized and cast into hell (19:11–20:10); the dead arise to be judged (20:11-15); and the New Jerusalem comes down from heaven (21:1–22:5).

A pause is inserted between the breaking of the sixth and the seventh seal. The 144,000 are sealed with the seal of God, and before the throne of God stands a multitude that no one can number (chap. 7). Again, two chapters are inserted between the blowing of the sixth and the seventh trumpets. John is told he must prophesy about the nations (chap. 10) and harsh words are said about the old Jerusalem (chap. 11). Another long exposition, inserted between the blowing of the seventh trumpet and the outpouring of the first bowl, makes it clear why the Roman empire must be destroyed: Rome is an instrument of the devil (chap. 12). Satan employs two accomplices: the beast from the sea and the beast out of the earth (chap. 13). Finally, a prelude to the great judgment is offered (chap. 14).

The praise songs serve an important function as inter-
mezzos. The four living creatures sing the threefold "holy"
(4:8) and the twenty-four elders praise God as the Creator
(4:11). When the Lamb takes the scroll he is addressed in
song, first alone (5:9-10, 12), then together with him who is
seated on the throne (5:13). The songs that follow have a strong
anticipatory character (7:10, 12; 11:15, 17-18; 12:10-12; 15:3-4;
19:1, 2, 5; 19:6-8). They anticipate victory.

VII. PROPHECY

John himself says that his work must be understood as prophecy, as we learn from both the prologue (1:3) and the epilogue
(22:7). He exhorts the copyists neither to add to nor to subtract
from his prophetic words (22:18-19). The vision of the angel
with the little scroll that John has to eat places him in the line
of Old Testament prophets. Just as Amos, Isaiah, Jeremiah,
and Ezekiel made prophetic pronouncements concerning different nations, so too John prophesies concerning many nations, peoples, languages, and kings (10:11).

As prophet, John makes frequent use of "the prophetic
perfect." An example may show what is meant by this "tense."
Babylon (Rome) has not yet fallen. Still, it is so certain that
this will happen that its fall can be proclaimed as having already happened. An angel cries out: "Fallen, fallen is Babylon
the great" (14:8). The sun still shines, but the barometer points
to stormy weather. Many of the praise songs are also proleptic
(anticipatory) in character. Voices in heaven say: the kingdom
of the world has become the kingdom of our Lord and of his
Christ (11:15), and the elders thank God that he has seized
power and begun to reign (11:17). The storm is still raging
but the barometer points to fine weather.

The difference between John and the prophets of the Old
Testament lies in the fact that Revelation has a strong chris-
tological foundation. There, too, lies the difference with Jewish apocalyptic. Only the Lamb may open the scroll having
the seven seals (5:5). The Lamb is conqueror in the war with
the beast and the ten kings (17:14). As the Rider on the white
horse, he defeats the beast, the kings, and their armies
(19:11-21).

This christocentricity is also the characteristic by which
one can tell the difference between true and false prophecy.

The false prophet (17:13; 19:20; 20:10) is the priestly profession that demands emperor-worship (13:11-18). True prophecy is the testimony to Jesus; it is the Spirit of prophecy (19:10). What the Spirit has to say to the churches (2:7, 11, 17, 29; 3:6, 13, 22) is that which Jesus has instructed John to write down concerning the churches in Asia (chaps. 2 and 3). In those churches, too, there is false prophecy in circulation: the doctrine of the Nicolaitans (2:6, 15), and a woman, a Jezebel, who says she is a prophetess (2:20). For that reason people should listen carefully to the Spirit, that is, to Jesus.

In the Greek church there was a long struggle over the question of whether or not to accept the Revelation of John in the canon. The Latin church had virtually no problem with it. (There the discussion centered around the Letter to the Hebrews.) For a long time the general epistles and Revelation were missing from the canon of the Syrian church. (There the conflict especially concerned the use of the Diatessaron in place of the four gospels.) In his series of commentaries on the books of the New Testament, Calvin omitted one on Revelation. Luther found the book neither apostolic nor prophetic. The teaching of justification by faith is not the only standard, however, for granting or denying the apostolic or prophetic character of a Bible book. John prophesies the downfall of Babylon (Rome) as an anti-God power. And that is a prophetic witness in the style of Isaiah, Jeremiah, Ezekiel, and Daniel.

VIII. LITERATURE

Barclay, W. *The Revelation of John.* The Daily Study Bible. 2 vols. 2d ed. Philadelphia: The Westminster Press, 1960.

Boer, H. R. *The Book of Revelation.* Grand Rapids: Wm. B. Eerdmans Publishing Co., 1979.

Beasley-Murray, G. R. *The Book of Revelation.* The New Century Bible Commentary. Edited by R. E. Clements and M. Black. Rev. ed. London: Marshall, Morgan & Scott, 1978. Reprint. Grand Rapids: Wm. B. Eerdmans Publishing Co., 1981.

Caird, G. B. *A Commentary on the Revelation of St. John the Divine.* Harper's New Testament Commentaries. New York: Harper & Row, 1966.

Charles, R. H. *A Critical and Exegetical Commentary on the Revelation of St. John.* The International Critical Commentary. 2 vols. Edinburgh: T. & T. Clark, 1920.

Collins, A. Y. *Apocalypse.* New Testament Message. New York: Michael Glazier, 1979.

Ellul, J. *Apocalypse: The Book of Revelation.* Translated by G. W. Schreiner. New York: Seabury Press, 1977.

Ladd, G. E. *A Commentary on the Revelation of John.* Grand Rapids: Wm. B. Eerdmans Publishing Co., 1972.

Morris, L. *The Revelation of St. John.* Tyndale New Testament Commentaries. Edited by R. V. G. Tasker. Grand Rapids: Wm. B. Eerdmans Publishing Co., 1969.

Mounce, R. H. *The Book of Revelation.* The New International Commentary on the New Testament. Edited by F. F. Bruce. Grand Rapids: Wm. B. Eerdmans Publishing Co., 1977.

Torrance, T. F. *The Apocalypse Today.* Grand Rapids: Wm. B. Eerdmans Publishing Co., 1959.

Wilcock, M. *I Saw Heaven Opened.* Downers Grove: InterVarsity Press, 1975.

PROLOGUE 1:1-8

1:1-3 HEADING

The subject matter concerns the revelation of "what must happen" in days to come. This term has been borrowed from the Book of Daniel (Dan. 2:28-29, 45). The future is hidden, known only to God. No one knows what he has decided in his counsel. But he can give a glimpse of it and confer insight into it. He has made known his plan to Jesus Christ. Jesus has passed on the contents of it to John by way of an angel. What John has seen through the mediation of the angel he must write down. This, in turn, has to be read publicly in the gatherings of the churches. The public reader and his hearers are congratulated in advance if they take to heart what John has written down. His book is prophecy: it has the weight of the words of the prophets of the Old Testament, the servants of God, to whom he has revealed his thoughts. And because the time of the end, fixed by God, is very close, it is important to pay extra attention to the revelation of John. The countdown has begun.

1:4-6 OPENING

Just as Paul does in his letters, John wishes the seven churches in Asia Minor grace and peace from God—he who is the God of past, present, and future. He is present; he was present; and he will come. The last statement is an Old Testament promise. God will come to dwell in the midst of his people (Ezek. 37:26-28; Zech. 2:10-11). This promise is fulfilled when the New Jerusalem comes down from heaven (21:3).

John also extends grace and peace from the seven spirits before God's throne. These spirits are the archangels, who stand like burning torches before the throne (4:5). They are the messengers who are sent forth over the whole earth (5:6): ministering spirits "for the sake of those who are to obtain salvation" (Heb. 1:14). Christ is Lord of the angels. He has

11

the seven spirits and the seven stars (the angels of the seven churches; 1:20) in his hand (3:1).

Further, John wishes grace and peace also from Jesus Christ, whom he adorns with titles of honor from Psalm 89. There David is called "the first-born," and "the highest of the kings of the earth" (Ps. 89:27). John, however, applies these titles to Jesus. It is one of the fundamental theses of Revelation that Jesus is superior to all earthly kings. The attribute "first-born" is here taken as the first who arose from the dead. In the psalm, God is "the faithful witness in the sky" (89:37) who promises David that his rule will last as long as the sun and moon are in the heavens. To John, Jesus is the faithful witness in heaven. Although the Greek word for witness does not yet have the later meaning of "martyr," John doubtless has in mind here a witness who died on the cross. The sequel also shows this.

Jesus loves us. He has redeemed us from our sins. His blood has washed away our iniquities. Thus he made us to be a kingdom of priests. Originally that was what Israel was to be (Exod. 19:6). Peter, though, applies these words to the church (1 Pet. 2:5, 9). For John this is an important point: that which concerns Israel is transferred to the church. (We shall run into this phenomenon repeatedly.) It is because of this love, redemption, and transfer of promise that Jesus must be praised "to the farthest ages." "The ages of the ages" is an expression in the superlative degree, as often occurs in the Hebrew. Other examples of this are "vanity of vanities" (the acme of vanity), "the song of songs" (the highest song), and "the king of kings" (the greatest king). And when in the churches the exhortation that Jesus be honored to the farthest ages is read, that must be answered with a resounding "Amen."

1:7-8 ANNOUNCEMENT OF THE THEME

John combines two passages from the Old Testament here: Daniel 7:13: ". . . and behold, with the clouds of heaven there came one like a son of man" and Zechariah 12:10ff.: ". . . when they look on him whom they have pierced, they shall mourn for him, as one mourns for an only child. . . . The land shall mourn, each family by itself." When Christ returns the Jews will see Jesus whom they had had crucified as a false

Messiah, whose heart a Roman soldier had pierced through
with a spear. When the Son of Man appears as Judge it is too
late to repent. Jews and Gentiles will be sorry that they have
not believed in him. The translation "they shall mourn for
him" does not fit here, because the Son of Man descending
on the clouds is not pitiable. Therefore it seems better to translate it: "With their eye on him they will raise a lament (over
themselves)."

God himself confirms that Jesus will come again and that
then there will be lamentation. The concluding words of
verse 7, "Even so. Amen," are not so much the response of
the church as the solemn introduction of an assurance from
the side of God. When they are allowed to function as the
start of verse 8 they acquire a much deeper meaning. The
division into verses is not the work of John. As far as that is
concerned, there can be no objection to a minor modification.
Thus, the Lord God is introduced as speaking: "Even so. Amen,
I am the Alpha and the Omega." He is the first and the last,
a position described with the first and last letter of the Greek
alphabet. He is the Lord, the God of hosts, Yahweh Sabaoth
(Hos. 12:6; Amos 3:13; 4:13; 5:14), reproduced in Greek by
"the Omnipotent." He who encompasses the ages, and is Lord
over all, guarantees the return of Jesus.

CALLING 1:9-20

The beginning "I John" is typical for the style of the seer of
the end of the world. That is also how Daniel spoke: "I, Daniel"; "I, your servant" [NIV] (Dan. 10:2, 7, 17). John, an exile
on the isle of Patmos, isolated from the churches, remains
their brother. He shares in their affliction. He shares the kingdom with them. Has not Jesus made them to be a kingdom
of priests (Rev. 1:6)? And with them he expects the return of
Jesus.

On the Lord's day, the day of the resurrection and of the
appearance of the Risen One, he receives a vision of an awesome human form. The description largely resembles that of
the man whom Daniel saw (Dan. 10:5-6), except that the head
and the hair, white as wool, white as snow, shows some resemblance to God, whose clothing was white as snow and
whose hair was white like wool (Dan. 7:9). By these touches

the author signifies that this person is more than human and more than the man whom Daniel saw. He shows some of the features of the Judge on his throne. And just as the Lord God made the mouth of the Servant of the Lord like a sharp sword (Isa. 49:2), so also the word proceeding out of the mouth of this mysterious man is razor-sharp. It will uncover and lay bare the deepest thoughts of the hearts of men (Heb. 4:12-13). The radiance of this Appearance is like the sun shining in all its brilliance.

When John fell on the ground as though dead, this terrifying Form made himself known. He placed his right hand on John and told him not to be afraid that he will die at seeing such intense majesty. It is the One crucified and risen who now touches him. The Living One did not come to kill but to liberate men from death. He has the keys to the gate of the realm of death and he rules forever as the First and the Last (a name for God; 1:8). For that reason John must write down not only what he saw (this he had been instructed to do earlier; 1:11) but also Christ's evaluation of the churches, and the things that will soon take place. That which is about to happen is a great mystery (10:7). But a small riddle can be solved immediately: the candlesticks represent the seven churches, and the seven stars are the angels of those churches. This presents a new riddle: Who or what is the angel of the church?

For an answer to that question it is necessary to point out the parallels between Revelation 1:9-20 and Daniel 10:2-20.

Revelation		*Daniel*	
1:9	I, John	10:2	I, Daniel
1:9-10	place and day: Patmos, Lord's Day	10:4	place and day: Tigris, 24th of the 1st month
1:13ff.	description of the Man	10:5-6	description of the man
1:17	John falls down as though dead	10:9	Daniel faints
1:17	The Man lays his hand on John	10:10	The man touches Daniel with his hand
1:17	Do not be afraid!	10:12	Do not be afraid!
1:19	Write down the things about to happen	10:14	Tell what will befall the people in the last days

1:20	the angels of the seven churches	10:13, 20-21	the angels who represent the nations

These similarities (in the same sequence!) are not accidental. For his description of the vision of his call John followed the model of Daniel 10. This gives us the clue to who or what the angels of the churches might be. In Daniel 10 there is reference to the angel representing the kingdom of Persia (vv. 13, 21). Greece, too, has its own angel (v. 20). They are prominent angels; hence the title "prince." The highest in rank is Michael, who champions the cause of Israel (Dan. 10:13, 21; 12:1). Similarly, each of the seven churches has its own angel as patron—analogous to the angels of the "little ones" (Matt. 18:10) and Peter's angel (Acts 12:15).

One problem remains: What connection is there between angels and stars? That connection is made by the word *prince*. Kings are often compared with stars. Balaam prophesied that a star would come forth out of Jacob and that a scepter would rise out of Israel (Num. 24:17). The star of Bethlehem showed the wise men from the East the way to the newborn king of the Jews (Matt. 2:2). In this light, it is not unusual to equate angels, having the rank of princes, with the stars.

Christ has the seven stars in his right hand (Rev. 1:16, 20). As Lord of the angels he is also the Head of those angels who maintain a special relationship with the seven churches in Asia Minor. The right hand symbolizes power and redemption. The right is the side of good fortune. On the day of judgment the sheep will be on the right side, the goats on the left (Matt. 25:33). Similarly, the seven stars in the right hand of Christ serve as encouragement to the churches. They (and we!) are in good hands.

SEVEN LETTERS 2:1–3:22

THE STRUCTURE OF THE LETTERS

John now proceeds to record "the things that are" (1:19). To that end he needs to write letters to the churches in the Roman province of Asia, the part of Asia Minor of which Ephesus was the center. These letters all have the same outline or structure.

1. The address is to the angel of the church in question. That presents a difficulty. Where does the mailman deliver the letter? We must not forget, however, that in a vision things can be done that are not considered possible otherwise. And just as John received the revelation of Jesus Christ through the mediation of an angel (1:1), so also the letter from Christ can be passed on by the angel who has a special tie with that church.

2. The opening statement is modeled on the introduction of prophetic utterances in the Old Testament: "Thus says the Lord." The letter starts out saying: "These are the words of him who . . ." and then harkens back to the characterizations of Jesus given in chapter 1 (except in the letter to the church in Philadelphia).

3. The content of the letter is comparable to a report of a church visitation. Each church is examined and judged by its "works"—a word translatable as "conduct of life," "behavior," "practices," "activities," or "achievements."

4. There is a call to pay adequate attention to the letter. The formula here reminds us of the statement in the gospels, "He who has ears to hear, let him hear" (e.g., Matt. 11:15). But there is an addition here: ". . . let him hear what the Spirit says to the churches." One must not, of course, play off Christ's words of praise or blame against what the Spirit says. What the Spirit has to say can be read in the letter from Christ. And what is written in a letter to one church must be read also in all the other churches (cf. Paul in Col. 4:16).

5. The promise is given to the one who wins the victory. The idea here is to bring the struggle to a good conclusion, to struggle on and persevere. The imagery is derived from the world of athletes (cf. 1 Cor. 9:24ff.; 2 Tim. 2:5; 4:7; Heb. 12:1-2).

6. The comfort and threat of the return of Jesus is emphasized. The theme of the prologue and the epilogue, "He is coming," "I am coming . . ." (1:7; 22:7, 12, 20) returns in all the letters. Jesus' coming is expressly referred to in six of the letters. Though it is not explicit in the second letter, there too it is very much assumed (2:10).

2:1-7 EPHESUS

The church at Ephesus is worthy of praise because it has unmasked pseudo-apostles. From the letter one cannot tell what these people taught. But the church is worthy of blame because it no longer loves as it did in the past. To put it in the words of Jeremiah, "I remember the devotion of your youth, your love as a bride" (Jer. 2:2). But that kind of spirituality has declined. If the church does not return to the earlier level, then Jesus, who is in the midst of the lampstands (1:13), will come to remove the lampstand of Ephesus from its place. In other words, Jesus himself will put an end to the existence of this church. That is a serious warning. Ephesus was an important church center. But without love a church is sounding brass, a clanging cymbal (1 Cor. 13:1). Is the theological scrutiny of itinerant preachers to be rejected? Ephesus hates the practices of the Nicolaitans (cf. the letter to Pergamum; 2:15), and Christ does, too. From this it is evident that theology serves a function. It takes deep insight to distinguish real apostles from pseudo-apostles.

The person who perseveres until the victory has been won will be allowed to eat from the tree of life, which is in Paradise. Whoever eats from that tree will live forever (Gen. 3:22). In Revelation that is the eternal life given by Jesus Christ.

2:8-11 SMYRNA

Not a word of criticism is addressed to the church at Smyrna. Hence there is no call to repentance either. Materially its members are poor, but from a spiritual point of view they are rich. (In Laodicea the case is directly opposite: there they are rich, but spiritually they are in the gutter [3:17].)

The Jews have made life difficult for Christians by spreading slander. The devil is behind it all. Things are only going to get worse: on the basis of false charges the government is going to imprison some members of the church. Just as Daniel and his friends were tested for ten days (Dan. 1:12, 14), so for ten days the devil gets a chance to see whether the faith of these Christians is genuine and real.

The sharp condemnation of the Jews is striking. They are not really Jews; they are a synagogue of Satan. This condemnation is reminiscent of the discussion between Jesus and the Jews about "having Abraham as father," where Jesus states that the devil is their father (John 8:44). "Synagogal fellowship of the Satan" is the reversal of Israel's title of honor as "the assembly of the Lord" or "the congregation of the Lord" (Num.

16:3; 20:4; 27:17; Josh. 22:16). An example of a similar conversion of a word into its opposite occurs in Hosea. The prophet calls Bethel (Hos. 12:4), where the Lord God appeared to Jacob in a dream (Gen. 28:16-19), "Beth-aven" (Hos. 4:15; 5:8; 10:5): not "house of God," but "house of sin," because Baal, and not the Lord God, was being served there.

In the face of the combined opposition of the Jews in Asia Minor and the Roman government, the crucial issue was that Christian believers must not deny the faith, holding fast at the cost of their lives if need be. The person remaining faithful will receive the crown of honor that belongs to eternal life. The winner received a wreath of laurels (1 Cor. 9:25; 2 Tim. 4:8; James 1:12; 1 Pet. 5:4). Thus death and life stood in opposition to each other. It is not by accident that at the outset Jesus introduced himself as "the First and the Last, who died and lived again," and so recalls the calling vision (1:17-18). Jesus knows what it means when Jews and Romans join in hostility. He promises the winner that he will remain outside of the domain of the second death. The wicked die twice. The second death (hellfire; Rev. 20:14; 21:8) inflicts horrible injuries. But that will not happen to those who persevere to the end.

2:12-17 PERGAMUM

Pergamum is typified as the place where Satan resides and where his throne is located. This characterization need not make us think only of the gigantic altar built to Zeus. Pergamum possessed many shrines, with temples for Athene, Asclepius, and Roma. The city was a center of Hellenistic culture and emperor-worship. Christians were not yet persecuted systematically, but one—Antipas—had already fallen victim. Like Jesus, he is called a faithful witness (1:5); the difference is that Jesus' death on the cross has atoning power and the martyrdom of Antipas was the price he paid for his fidelity to the gospel. Jesus praises the church of Pergamum for not denying the faith even when it saw to what end this could lead.

But he accuses the church of having members who hold to the doctrine of the Nicolaitans, which is the same as that of Balaam. Israel allowed itself to be seduced into taking part in a sacrificial feast of the Moabites, a religious fertility-rite that ended in sexual intercourse (Num. 25:1-2). This took place on the advice of Balaam (Num. 31:16), who, knowing the Israelites' weak spot, had advised Balak to try to tempt them with a festive sacrifice. The doctrine of the Nicolaitans comes down to the same thing. To Paul there was no fundamental objection to eating meat that had been sacrificed (1 Cor. 8:4-13); still, the practice was not as innocent as it seemed. Jesus takes it very ill of the church of Pergamum that it has not dealt with this issue. In the very place where Antipas remained faithful at the price of his life, the church neglects to exercise discipline over those who follow the advice of Balaam. The church must repent. In any case, Christ, who has the sharp two-edged sword (cf. 1:16), will fight with the sword of his mouth and, with the breath of his lips, will slay the wicked (Isa. 11:4).

To those who hold fast to the name of Christ he will give manna to eat: the food of life in the age to come. This manna, however, is "hidden." It was given to Israel on its wanderings through the wilderness and comes down like bread from heaven. That is, no one has it in his own power. It is now with God and will become manifest after the great victory of God and the Lamb.

To each of the winners is also given a white stone on which his or her new name is written. This new name is known only to the person who receives it. In the same way also Christ, the Rider on the white horse, has a name that no one knows but himself (19:12). There are a number of interpretations of the white stone, but none of them is completely satisfactory. White is the color of heaven and eternal bliss. It is a common Oriental ideal that upon entering a new situation a person should have a new name. Reference has also been made to the fact that Jerusalem will get a new name, presently unknown, but fixed by God (Isa. 62:2). Nevertheless, it remains unclear why the new name should be inscribed on a white stone. Is it a nontransferable ticket of admission to the kingdom of glory?

2:18-29 THYATIRA

Jesus, the Son of God (the only time this title occurs in Revelation!) praises this church because, in contrast with Ephesus, the level of its spiritual life is showing improvement. But he has one big objection: it lets a woman who passes herself off as a prophetess do as she pleases. This woman belongs to the Nicolaitan party (Rev. 2:6, 15) and teaches *à la* Balaam: eat food offered to idols and commit immorality (2:14). She is a deceiver and John has but one name for her: Jezebel, wife of Ahab, mother of Joram, of whom Jehu said, "What peace can there be so long as the harlotries and sorceries of your mother Jezebel are so many?" (2 Kings 9:22). She refuses to repent although Jesus gave her the opportunity. For that reason the so-called prophetess will get sick; the people she seduced will, unless they repent, suffer terribly; those who remain with her will die of the plague. This will make a strong impression on the churches. They will acknowledge that he, whose eyes blaze like fire (cf. 1:14) and consume impurity, searches the minds and hearts of people (Ps. 7:9; Jer. 11:20; 17:10; 20:12). And he, whose feet burn away unholiness like a stream of white-hot ore (cf. 1:15), will repay each one according to what he has done (Ps. 62:12; Rev. 22:12).

And what does Jesus require now of those church members who have not, as they claim, learned to know the unfathomable depths of God, but rather the abysmal depths of Satan? Only to hold fast to what they have till Christ returns. Earlier, Revelation changed "the assembly of God" into its opposite, "the synagogue of Satan" (2:9; 3:9). The same thing happens here with "the depths of God" accessible only to the Spirit (1 Cor. 2:10); in fact, they are busy looking into the dizzying depths of Satan. By letting oneself be induced to take part in the sacrificial feasts and sacred immorality one does not arrive at a deeper knowledge of God but only becomes thoroughly acquainted with Satan.

Those who overcome this temptation will receive the same power over the nations that God, in accordance with Psalm 2:9, has given to his Son. Perhaps this is the reason why, in the beginning of this letter, Jesus is called the Son of God (2:18). As the promised messianic king he will not rule the nations with the shepherd's crook but with an iron rod (12:5; 19:15). He will lash out at them and break them to pieces like fragile pottery. Those who achieve victory will settle accounts, alongside the Conqueror, with the enemies.

The symbol of royal rule is the morning star, the planet Venus. Venus was the mother of Aeneas, who fled burning Troy and landed in Italy. She was the grandmother of Julius,

the son of Aeneas. Thus Venus is the matriarch of the re-
nowned Roman patrician family from which Julius Caesar and
Caesar Augustus descended. Venus was the national goddess
of the Romans, and was named "Victrix"—female conqueror.
It is not the emperor in Rome who is the world ruler, however,
but Christ, the glittering star of the morning (22:16). And
those who are his will rule with him as kings (5:10; 20:4, 6;
22:5). He who conquers will sit with Christ on his throne
(3:21). The sign of this is that he will give to him the morning
star (2:28).

3:1-6 SARDIS

The church at Smyrna could be described as "poor—yet rich."
Similarly, the church at Sardis has the reputation of being
alive—but is dead. It puts up a big front but does not meet
the standards that God applies. Not all the members of this
church are spiritually dead, but unless they receive restora-
tives soon, they too will die. There is but one remedy: return
to the gospel as they have received it and have heard it in the
beginning. It is past high time that this church, which has
fallen asleep, should awaken. Christ will come as a thief and
you do not know when (Matt. 24:43-44; Luke 12:39-40; 1 Thess.
5:2, 4; 2 Pet. 3:10). The person who does not take off his
clothes at night (16:15) is to be congratulated, for Jesus could
come in the wee hours.

Fortunately there are exceptions to the prevailing dismal
rule in the church. There are those who have not soiled their
clothes. It is not so strange that people have linked this language with sexual impurity: Nicolas, Balaam, and Jezebel have
made their conquests in three out of seven churches (2:6,
14-15, 20). One may also recall the filthy clothes worn by the
high priest Joshua (Zech. 3:3). In the context, however, dirty
clothes have no connection with illegitimate sexual behavior.
There are other ways to get dirty in this world. The clean
members of the church have kept the commandments of God
(12:17; 14:12), which has earned them the white clothes of the
inhabitants of heaven (3:18; 4:4; 6:11; 7:9, 13; 19:14).

The one who wins a victory is given the guarantee that
Christ will not erase his or her name from the book of life.
That is a familiar biblical way of picturing things. When a
person's name was crossed out, he died (Exod. 32:32-33; Ps.

21

69:28). In later years the book of life became the register of the names of people who would inherit eternal life (Dan. 12:1; Luke 10:20; Phil. 4:3; Rev. 20:12; 21:27). Those whose names were not in the book would go to destruction (13:8; 17:8; 20:5).

When the book of life is opened (20:12) and the names are read out loud, Jesus will declare before God his Father and his angels that the names of those who have overcome were rightly recorded in that book. That is the act of confession by which Jesus rewards the people who have confessed his name (Matt. 10:32; Luke 12:8). The reference to angels takes us back to the beginning of this letter. Then follows, as always, a reminder of chapter 1. Christ holds in his hands both the seven spirits of God, the archangels who stand before his throne (1:4), and the seven stars, the angels who represent the seven churches (1:20). There is every reason to take him seriously. Whoever has ears, use them!

3:7-13 PHILADELPHIA

As he addresses the church at Philadelphia, Jesus speaks of himself as the Holy and True One. This is also what he is called as the Rider on the white horse (19:11). God himself is addressed in the same terms by the souls under the altar (6:10). So that is one of the ways in which the God-likeness of Jesus is expressed and his equality with God is underscored.

As a rule there is a link between the opening statement of a letter and the vision of John's calling in chapter 1. That is not the case here. A few manuscripts force a connection by substituting the key of Hades for the key of David (1:18). But that is clearly a correction of the text. The key of David is a symbol for authority over the house of David in Isaiah 22:22. In Revelation it is the Messiah who has the key to the gate of the New Jerusalem. He decides who is to be admitted and who remains outside.

But Jesus also opens other doors. A miracle will happen: a number of Jews will come to the church, bow down deeply, and acknowledge that God loves the church. It is natural to think of Jesus as the subject of the sentence "I love you." But it takes no special acknowledgment to admit the fact that Jesus loves his church. The sentence in question is, after all, a quotation (Isa. 43:3). A number of Jews have come to understand that the Lord God loves the church of Jesus. That which was utterly unthinkable for the Jews, namely, that the God of Israel would love the congregation of a false Messiah, is here accepted. Therein lies the core of the acknowledgment. They, therefore, are the true Jews. The other Jews are no Jews, and they lie if they say that they are Jews (cf. Rev. 2:9).

Jesus gives the true Jews to the church as a present in reward for their faithfulness. The church of Philadelphia has not denied his name. Financially the church may not represent much. They have little "strength," a word that repeatedly means "possessions." One who loves God cannot keep his wallet shut (Mark 12:30, 33). Although this church cannot be highly regarded on account of its money and wealth, Jesus is full of praise for it. It is characteristic that the call to repentance is not to be found in this letter. That was true also for the church at Smyrna—another small congregation (2:9), which, remarkably, was also burdened with the existence of "a synagogue of Satan" (2:9).

Jesus rewards this little church: because it has faithfully kept the command of Jesus to keep looking for his return, he will keep this church during the severe test to which the entire world will be subject. To examine is to draw out the stuff that is in a person (ex-agimen). People are tested on their external quality and inner stamina. The congregation will not be spared this test. It is kept in, not from, the time of trouble. The multitude that no one can number comes out of the great tribulation (7:14). Precisely what this refers to is not explained, although there is an allusion to Daniel's prediction, "There will be a time of distress such as has not happened from the beginning of nations" (Dan. 12:1). There is a general expectation that hard times will precede the coming of God's kingdom (Acts 14:22). The Jews call these "the messianic pains." What that means may be discovered by reading Matthew 24:1-28; Mark 13:1-23; Luke 21:5-28. No one else will get the crown of laurels destined for the members of the church, and therefore they must hold on to what they have (cf. Rev. 2:25). The time of testing will not be long: Jesus will come soon.

He who is victorious will get a statue in the temple of God. The idea of a pillar or a column that will never leave presents problems. The removal of a pillar results in the collapse of the roof. It is better to suppose that this is an allusion to a bust that the high priest of the imperial temple commissioned for himself. Carved into it were his name, his father's name and city, and the year of his administration. The high priest was in office for one year. His successor, after his year of service, also placed a memorial column in the temple. In the end there were so many that the sculptured images of the less popular figures were removed. They had to go. Against this background the text lights up. On the conqueror's statue the name of God, the name of the city of God, and the new name of Christ will be inscribed. And when he who holds the key of David has admitted his own in the New Jerusalem, they will never leave again. They bear the new name of Christ (19:12) and are therefore clearly marked as his possession. The polemic undercurrent is unmistakable. The memorial pillar does not bear one's own name, nor that of the earthly father, nor that of his birthplace, nor the year of service. *Soli Deo Gloria!*

3:14-22 LAODICEA

In this letter Jesus introduces himself as "the Amen," the only instance in the New Testament where "amen" occurs as a noun. In the Old Testament God is the God of the amen (see Hebrew text, Isa. 65:16): One can count on him. Similarly, Jesus, as God's amen, is faithful and true.

The translation "the beginning of God's creation" (RSV) seems to me infelicitous. If Jesus was created first, like Wisdom in the Book of Proverbs (Prov. 8:22), he is and remains a creature: first among his equals. That is not in harmony with the Christology of Revelation, which repeatedly stresses Jesus' equality with God. Therefore, the translation "the origin of God's creation" deserves preference. Jesus took part in the work of the Creator (John 1:3; Col. 1:15ff.) and was there before creation. One may not worship a creature; that honor belongs exclusively to God (19:10) and to the Lamb (5:13).

The letter does not have a good word to say about Laodicea; it is exceptionally sharp. To be spat out, like a mouthful of lukewarm water, is a harsh judgment. Laodicea claims to resemble Ephraim (Hosea 12:8), which has everything and needs nothing. But when Christ examines the church of Laodicea it is evident that it has nothing and needs everything. Wretched, pitiable, poor, blind, naked—the words are heaped up to bring to light its really wretched condition.

Jesus advises this city of bankers to buy from him the

real gold. He advises this city of textile products to buy from him the white clothes of purity and victory, for despite the most costly clothing in their possession, they have nothing on and are going about naked. And this city of apothecaries would do well to buy from him an eye salve to cure them of their blindness. All this advice is a last effort to bring Laodicea to conversion. The background is love: hence the quotation from the Book of Proverbs (Prov. 3:12), also cited in the Epistle to the Hebrews (Heb. 12:6).

Jesus is not optimistic. When he returns he will come to the churches (Rev. 2:5, 16, 25; 3:3, 11)—only in the case of Laodicea, he appeals to the individual! He knocks on the door. If there is no response, he goes on his way. If someone opens, there is a feast. To eat together is to create fellowship, which has a covenantal character. As a rule Jesus' act of standing by the door and knocking is interpreted as the knock on the door of a person's heart. A comparison with a passage like Luke 12:36-37 suggests an eschatological context. Luke uses the same images: to come, knock, open, eat. These all relate to Christ's return.

The one who is victorious will be allowed to sit next to Jesus on his throne. The promise to rule with Christ is one that is made often (Rev. 1:6; 5:10; 20:6; 22:5; cf. Luke 22:29-30; 2 Tim. 2:12). Note the parallel here: "as I myself conquered and sat down with my Father on his throne." Christ's victory was his death on the cross. He has run the race, gained the victory, and received the reward (Heb. 12:1-2). For that reason he is the faithful Witness. The conclusion of the letter to the church at Laodicea corresponds with the beginning and at the same time reaches back to the initial address of chapter 1 (1:5).

SEVEN SEALS 4:1–6:17

Following the assurance that the victor will be allowed to sit with Christ on his throne, as Christ now sits by his Father on his (3:21), the throne of God is now pictured (chap. 4). In his right hand God holds a scroll whose content is a secret. In it are recorded future events, which can be initiated only by the breaking of the seven seals. Only the Lamb is authorized to do this (chap. 5). Next, the seals are broken open one by one—with all of the consequences of this act (chap. 6).

4:1-11 THE THRONE

After the first vision, in which John saw the glorified Christ, there now follows a second. Again he falls into ecstasy (1:10; 4:2). Again he hears the mysterious voice (1:10; 4:1). He will now be shown what must happen soon (1:1, 19; 4:1). To that end a door is opened in heaven: a privilege extended only to a few individuals (Jacob [Gen. 28:17]; Ezekiel [Ezek. 1:1]; John the Baptist [Matt. 3:16]; the disciples [John 1:51]; Stephen [Acts 7:56]; and Peter [Acts 10:11]). John is invited to come up. In the Spirit he ascends and sees a throne, which is clearly the throne of God. But John expresses himself as vaguely as possible. Isaiah saw the Lord on his throne (Isa. 6:1); Ezekiel saw "a likeness as it were of a human form" (Ezek. 1:26); John sees something that glitters like precious stones, and around the throne a halo green as emerald. The Greek word *iris* does not necessarily mean "rainbow"; a rainbow the color of emerald would be a rainbow of only one color. Hence the translation "halo."

John is afraid to describe God; so he uses the expression "He who sits on the throne" (4:3, 9-10; 5:1, 7, 13; 6:16; 7:15b; 20:11; 21:5), which serves to avoid the name of God. This was common practice by Jews out of fear of violating the third commandment. John does not follow it consistently, however, for the odd time we read: "God, who sits on the throne" (Rev. 7:10, 15a; 19:4).

Around the throne were put twenty-four thrones on which twenty-four elders were seated, clothed in white and crowned with gold. They constitute the heavenly retinue: a picture to be found in several places in the Old Testament (1 Kings 22:19; Job 1:6; 2:1; Ps. 89:7; Dan. 7:9-10). They are called elders because of the prophecy that the Lord will manifest his glory "before his elders" (Isa. 24:23). There is probably an astrological background to the fact that they number twenty-four: the twelve signs of the zodiac, plus the seven planets, plus five other constellations. It is no accident that the Greek alphabet, from the alpha to the omega, has twenty-four letters. More important is the fact that these twenty-four elders do not serve as councillors with whom the Lord consults concerning his plans. They exist only to sing his praises!

From the throne issue flashes of lightning, voices, and peals of thunder. These "voices" are to be understood as the noise of wind gusts accompanying the thunderstorms. They are natural phenomena that come with the revelation of God and underscore his impressive majesty. That is how it was on Mt. Sinai (Exod. 19:16). The Greek translation of Exodus 20:18 adds flaming torches to that scene. Nor are they lacking before the throne in this vision. John interprets them as the seven spirits of God, the seven archangels (1:4; 3:1; 5:6).

In front of the throne stretched a clear expanse of crystalline sea. This feature derives from the image of the earth floating on the primeval ocean like a flat disc. But there is another ocean, one surrounding the vault of heaven (Pss. 104:3; 148:4), the firmament that separated the watery masses above from those below (Gen. 1:6ff.).

In the midst of and surrounding the throne were four living creatures. They tended, in turn, to resemble a lion, a bull, an animal with a human face, and an eagle in flight. Originally they were the four signs of the zodiac. The eyes with which these animals are dotted in front and behind point in an astrological direction. Those "eyes" are stars that sparkle in the sky. In Ezekiel the four living creatures support the throne of God (Ezek. 1); in John's revelation that is not the case.

One may question how these four living creatures could be simultaneously in the center and around the throne [cf. NIV]. The phenomenon can be explained as follows: On the one hand, the celestial canopy itself is regarded as the throne of God (Isa. 66:1; Matt. 5:34; 23:22; Acts 7:49); on the other, the throne of God is situated in the center of the canopy. One could say—cryptically—the throne God is located in the throne of God. Less cryptically, we could say the throne of God is located in the throne room. This is how the four living creatures can be both in the center of, and around, the throne of God. This fits the style of apocalyptic literature in which images often melt into each other.

Colors run through each other here—as can be seen also from the four living creatures. John freely uses Ezekiel's description of the appearance of the glory of God. From that vision he borrows the lion, the bull, the animal with a human face, and the eagle (Ezek. 1). This he combines with Isaiah's vision, in which each of the seraphs around the throne of God had six wings (Isa. 6:2). The thrice "holy" also derives from this vision (Isa. 6:3). The fact that they praise God day and night without pause and that their wings inside and out are full of eyes is to be attributed to what John himself has seen. In addition, the expansion "who is, and who was, and who is to come" (cf. Rev. 1:4, 8) is John's own.

Each time the four living creatures sing out the "holy, holy, holy," the twenty-four elders cast themselves down in adoration before God and throw their crowns down in front of the throne as a sign of acknowledgment that God alone is entitled to glory and honor. Thus, in the liturgy of heaven, the four living creatures antiphonally praise the holiness of God while the twenty-four elders praise God as Creator. It should not escape us that the twenty-four elders address God as "Our Lord and God." In Latin, that is "Dominus et Deus noster"—the official title by which the Roman emperor Domitian arrogated divine honors for himself. This is the first allusion to, and the first repudiation of, emperor-worship, a theme that gains ever sharper contours in Revelation. Around this theme, and in this polemic, the conflict between church and state takes shape.

5:1-14 THE SCROLL THAT IS SEALED

After the description of the throne of God with the seven archangels, the four living creatures, and the twenty-four elders who surround it, the moment has come for John to be shown the things that "must take place." That future, recorded on a scroll, is so full of events that the parchment is covered with writing on both sides. This fact by itself is indicative of something special; it was extremely unusual for both sides of the paper to be used. The scroll that Ezekiel had to eat had the same characteristic (Ezek. 2:10).

The scroll is sealed with seven seals—an indication that the contents are to be considered "Top Secret" (cf. Dan. 12:4, 9). For people to be able to read the scroll the seals have to be broken. But who has permission to do that? It appears that in the entire universe (note the tripartite division: heaven, earth, and the world below) there is no one who can be considered worthy and fit for this act. The question of the mighty angel—

it had to be an announcer with enormous vocal power so that his cry could sound in the remotest corners of creation—remained unanswered. For that reason John burst into tears. Is there no one, then, who can put the plan of God into effect? For, in this case, to read the scroll is to carry out the contents.

One of the elders comforts him, saying, "Do not cry. There is One who is worthy: Jesus, the Messiah, the Lion from Judah's tribe. He has been promised the kingship (Gen. 49:9-10). He is David's descendant. Around his banner the nations will rally (Isa. 11:1, 10). On the cross he was victorious."

Then, in the throne room between the living creatures and the elders, John discovers a Lamb (cf. John 1:29, 36). It is slain (Isa. 53:7), and the wounds are still visible. But the Lamb is *standing*. The One who was crucified is risen. The seven horns symbolize strength (Dan. 7:20ff.; 8:3ff.; Rev. 17:3ff.). And the seven eyes? In the prophet Zechariah they are symbols of the omniscience of God (Zech. 4:10); in John they represent the archangels (Rev. 1:4; 3:1; 4:5) who have been sent out over the whole world. The fact that the Lamb has seven eyes means that he has the special messenger of God at his disposal—he and no one else.

The Lamb went and took the scroll out of the hand of God. As he did so the four living creatures and the elders fell down before the Lamb and thus offered him the same honor they gave to God (4:10).

The elders have bowls filled with incense in their hands. This indicates that the prayers of the believers have penetrated into heaven, and fulfills the Psalmist's prayer, "Let my prayer be counted as incense before thee" (Ps. 141:2). The elders have caught these prayers and so believers are comforted, for their prayers have not blown away in the wind (cf. 8:3). Another form of encouragement is that they are called "saints." They belong to "the people of the saints of the Most High" (Dan. 7:18, 22, 27) to whom an eternal kingdom has been promised. They will reign on earth (5:10; 22:5).

Also in the hands of the elders are harps. With these instruments they accompany their song—a new song. It is hard to tell whether they do this jointly with the four living creatures or alone. Of more importance is the fact that it is a "new" song (Pss. 33:3; 40:3; 98:1; 144:9; Isa. 42:10). But songs have always been sung. What is so new about this? The new element is that the singing concerns Jesus and his work. That is in agreement with the Jewish expectation that a new song will be raised in the days of the Messiah. By his sacrificial death on the cross the Lamb has acquired, for God, from all the nations, a people who will be a kingdom of priests (1:6; 20:6). Because the Lamb has been slain, he is the only one entitled to break the seals of the scroll. As concerns their liturgical form, the words sung in praise of the Lamb can be found in 1 Chronicles 29:11.

The circle of singers grows ever larger. In the innermost circle are the four living creatures; around them are the elders; then come innumerable angels. And the outermost circle includes all living beings in creation. All this John hears and sees in heaven. But how are things on earth?

6:1-8 THE BREAKING OF THE FOUR SEALS

When the Lamb breaks the first seal open, and at the command of one of the living creatures, there appears a white horse, its rider an archer. He has already gained the victory. God has given him a crown of laurels and so he will conquer. The passive form of the verb ("was given") is a typically Jewish way of avoiding the name of God in order not to violate the third commandment.

This rider on the white horse is not the same as the one in Revelation 19:11ff. There it is Jesus Christ; here it is the representative of the Parthians who continually threaten the Roman Empire.

The second rider, sitting on a bright red horse, symbolizes war—hence that big sword. And this war will lead to civil war.

The third rider, sitting on the black horse, signifies famine. Because of the war there will be a shortage of food, driving up food prices. A denarius is a small Roman silver coin. Whatever is scarce becomes expensive, and the black market flourishes. Food products are rationed—suggested by the scales—as in the time of Ezekiel when, during the siege of Jerusalem, bread and water were provided in fixed portions (Ezek. 4:16). Some will also tamper with oil and wine, adding liquids to increase the quantity but decrease the quality. A mysterious voice—is it the voice of God?—forbids this.

The fourth rider, sitting on the pale horse, is Death—trailing Hades (the abode of the dead) behind him. His color is appropriate: a deathly pale. Judgment passes over the world and punishment is carried out as in Ezekiel: sword, famine, wild beasts, and the plague (Ezek. 14:21). A quarter of the human population dies. Soon it will be a third (8:7–9:21), and so it will go until the end comes (14:14-20).

This vision of the four apocalyptic horsemen reminds one of the night visions of Zechariah (Zech. 1:8; 6:1-8). John makes his own use of them, however: the colors of the horses differ, and so does their function. One could say it is a free elaboration—in the spirit of what Jesus said in his speech about the last things (Matt. 24:6ff.; Mark 13:7ff.; Luke 21:10-11).

6:9-11 THE BREAKING OF THE FIFTH SEAL

The breaking of the fifth seal calls attention to the martyrs. John sees their souls under the altar. The fact that there should be an altar in heaven is not so unusual when we know that already in early times the earthly sanctuary was viewed as a replica of a heavenly original. Moses had to make a tabernacle on the pattern shown him on the mountain (Exod. 25:9, 40; 26:30; Heb. 8:5). John repeatedly refers to the heavenly altar (8:3, 5; 9:13; 14:18; 16:7). At the time of the opening of the scroll the altar is the place where the souls of the martyrs reside. This is why in later ages the churches buried under the altar the saints who had died, and kept their relics there: they followed the heavenly example.

John hears the martyrs cry aloud. They are becoming impatient. How long must they still wait for the day when God will avenge their death and the inhabitants of the earth? The fact that God will not leave the blood of his servants unavenged is well established elsewhere (Deut. 32:43; 2 Kings 9:7). In John's Revelation, judgment strikes not only the immediate murderers but all people. He often uses the expression "those who inhabit the earth" (3:10; 6:10; 8:13; 11:10; 13:8, 12, 14; 17:2, 8). The whole world is in a state of rebellion against God. Those who proclaim the Word of God, obey the commandments, and hold to the testimony of Jesus (1:2, 9; 12:17; 19:10) are victimized by this rebellion.

The question of the martyrs, familiar also to the Old Testament (Ps. 79:6; Zech. 1:12), is understandable. How long? The answer is that it will not be long. There will be still more believers who will die a martyr's death, but there will not be more, neither will there be fewer, than God has determined. Until the number God has fixed is reached they must rest—rest from their labor (14:13)—and be patient until the day of their eternal destination (Dan. 12:13). To each of them is given a long white robe as a pledge that their share in salvation is secure.

To avoid misunderstanding it may be useful to comment on the word *soul*. Almost automatically we tend to think it refers to disembodied immortal souls. But that can hardly be the case here. The souls call out aloud from under the altar and are dressed in white clothes. "Soul," in Hebrew, refers to a living being and can be used both of people and animals. It is also used for the dead who can still be identified, before the body has decomposed (Lev. 19:28; 22:4; Num. 5:2; 9:6, 10; 19:13; Hag. 2:13). In the various translations, "the dead," "the dead body," or "corpse" have taken the place of the word "soul."

6:12-17 THE BREAKING OF THE SIXTH SEAL

The breaking of the sixth seal graphically depicts the day for which the souls under the altar have called. The forerunners are catastrophes in nature as these have been predicted by the prophets (Isa. 13:10; 34:4; 50:3; Ezek. 32:7; Joel 2:30-31) and also proclaimed by Jesus (Matt. 24:7, 29; Mark 13:8, 24-25; Luke 21:11, 25-26). An enormous earthquake takes place. The smoke of an active volcano turns the sun as black as goat-hair cloth and the moon as red as blood. Stars fall from the sky like unripe fruit from a tree. The firmament is rolled up—we would say—like a carpet. Mountains and islands are hurled from their places.

This outbreak of chaos produces panic among the people. Rank or standing no longer matter. All people, high and low, look for caves and caverns (Isa. 2:19), wishing they could be crushed in an instant by falling blocks of stone (Hos. 10:8; Luke 23:30). Better to be dead than to face the wrath of God and the Lamb! "Who can stand before his indignation? Who can endure the heat of his anger?" (Nah. 1:6). The Old Testament only knows of the wrath of God; Revelation adds to that the wrath of the Lamb. It is "their wrath"—a remarkable expression. In this respect also Jesus is equal to God. And this twofold wrath is altogether unbearable.

THE 144,000 AND THE MULTITUDE NO ONE CAN COUNT 7:1-17

Before the seventh seal is broken John inserts a pause. The answer to the question "Who can stand the double outpouring of wrath?" can be only that no one will be able to maintain himself or herself on that daunting day. But before the storm breaks loose, the 144,000 receive the imprint of the seal of the living God on their forehead as a sign that they will be spared. After that John sees an innumerable multitude from all lands and peoples before God's throne. They have fought the battle and won. So they are dressed in white and carry palm branches in their hands. The wrath of God and of the Lamb is not directed against those who have let themselves be cleansed by the blood of Christ.

7:1-8 THE 144,000

Four angels standing at the four corners of the earth are ready to release the stormwinds. They are called the four "winds of the earth": the North, South, East, and West winds. They will cause enormous damage on earth, on the sea, and in the trees. But the angels must wait until the servants of God are sealed. The "sealing" process is inspired by the prophet Ezekiel. Those who will be spared in the coming judgment are first marked (Ezek. 9). The believers in the Book of Revelation receive an impression of a seal on their forehead. They will survive the judgment. As it appears from 14:1, this impression consists of the names of the Lamb and of God; by it they will be marked as the possession of the Father and the Son.

They number 144,000. That is not a literal figure, as can easily be seen from the schematism used: from every tribe of Israel, large or small, there will be the same 12,000. Thus, it is a sacred number (for more detail, see the Introduction to this book). Anyone wanting to take it literally must take care that his church does not fall below, or exceed, that number. If one is short a few numbers, one has to proselytize. If one has too many, he must try to get rid of a few.

The 144,000 represent a distinct group of Christians. They are the same people John saw standing with the Lamb on Mount Zion. They are the first people of the human race to be redeemed. To be able to follow the Lamb they refrained from marriage. In other regards, too, they are spotless. Only they are allowed to hear the new song that is sung in heaven (14:1-5). They constitute a select group. And this elite is the true people of God. For that reason these marked ones come out of the twelve tribes of Israel. James views Christians as the twelve tribes in the dispersion (James 1:1). Peter does the same thing (1 Pet. 1:1). John applies it to the best of the militia of Christ. That is not to say they are without sin. They, too, were redeemed by the blood of the Lamb. But there is a difference. The intensity of faith, hope, and love is not the same in all Christians.

It seems to me to be most improbable that John had in mind Jews who believed in Christ. His judgment on Jews is exceptionally sharp. Those who lie by saying they are Jews are not Jews. They are a synagogue of Satan. It is only an unusual individual who will join the church of Jesus Christ (Rev. 2:9; 3:9). Jerusalem itself is called Sodom and Egypt (11:8).

Anyone checking out the twelve tribes in Revelation can discover that one tribe is missing and that one name in the series does not belong. In Jacob's farewell to his sons, the tribe of Dan is compared with a snake (Gen. 49:17). For John that is the old serpent, the devil, the satan, the dragon (12:9)—and therefore unusable. But if one tribe is left out, another name must be found to make the number twelve complete. For that purpose John takes Manasseh, Joseph's oldest son. He might also have chosen Ephraim, the youngest son, who was blessed by Jacob in preference to the oldest one (Gen. 48:8-22). It stands to reason that Judah should be first in the lineup, for out of the tribe of Judah the Messiah was to come (Gen. 49:10).

7:9-17 THE MULTITUDE NO ONE CAN COUNT

Following the vision of the sealing of the 144,000, John sees a multitude no one can number. No army is composed of crack troops only: besides them, there are also soldiers who did not stand out and have won no special distinction. That is a comfort for the many Christians who are not distinguished by extraordinary courage. The people of God do not consist only of heroes. In all nations God has simple believers who have remained faithful. And just as the descendants of Abraham cannot be numbered (Gen. 15:5), so the number of Christians cannot be calculated. We do have our statistics— but they are based exclusively on external characteristics: church attendance, participation in the Lord's Supper, children in church school, financial contributions, and the like. That can hardly be otherwise. John sees the blessed before the throne of God, in white, holding palm branches as signs of victory and conquest. We have only the data of the church militant—not of the church triumphant.

The vision of the multitude that cannot be numbered serves to encourage the church. It will endure the storms that will make havoc of the world. John is permitted to see the things that God has prepared for those who love him (1 Cor. 2:9). They thank God and the Lamb for their rescue. Angels say amen to it, hurl themselves down and glorify God. When this doxological statement is read in the churches, believers on earth will also assent to it with their "amens."

To make clear why the saved are in heaven the question-and-answer method is applied. Question: Who are they and where did they come from? Answer: "Sir, you know." Then follows the explanation. The same thing happened in the case of the prophet Ezekiel (Ezek. 37:3), and a similar dialogue occurs in Zechariah 4.

The saved have not had an easy time of it on earth. Behind them they have the great tribulation that Daniel predicted (Dan. 12:1), to which also Jesus refers (Matt. 24:21; Mark 13:19) and which was mentioned before (3:10). In words that echo the prophecy concerning Judah who will "wash his garments in wine and his robes in the blood of grapes" (Gen. 49:11) and allude to Isaiah's statement that "though your sins be as scarlet they shall be white as snow; though they be red like crimson, they shall be as wool" (Isa. 1:18), one of the elders expresses the paradox: they have washed their garments and made them white in the blood of the Lamb. By Jesus' death on the cross he has atoned for their sins and they have been reconciled (cf. 2 Cor. 5:18-21).

Therefore they will share in the fulfillment of Old Testament promises: God will dwell among them (Ezek. 37:26ff.; Zech. 2:10-11); they will suffer neither hunger nor thirst, neither sun stroke nor heat, but dwell in an oasis (Isa. 49:10); there will be springs that do not dry up; their tears will be wiped away (Isa. 25:8). All this will compensate for the persecution they have suffered. In the concluding vision the same promises return (21:3, 4, 6).

Four angels stood ready to release the stormwinds (7:1). But they never received the command to do it. John does not return to the subject. Other catastrophes are on the way.

THE BREAKING OF THE SEVENTH SEAL 8:1-5

When the Lamb breaks open the seventh seal, heaven holds its breath. Tension increases almost beyond the point of endurance. Now the martyrs will be avenged (6:10). Seven angels stand ready to sound the final trumpet (1 Cor. 15:52; 1 Thess. 4:16; Matt. 24:31). During this brief half hour of silence the prayers of all the saints are brought before God. An angel places the incense, together with the prayers, on the golden altar before the throne, and the smoke of the incense, together with the prayers, rises up to God.

Earlier (5:8) the prayers of the saints were compared with incense; here they are mixed with incense. In neither case is anything said about the contents of the prayers. But they must have been concerned with judgment. That is evident from the response: fire on earth, thunder and lightning, storms and an earthquake. It is the same combination of natural phenomena that is in Isaiah 29:6.

There is a striking resemblance here between Revelation and the prophecies of Ezekiel. In Ezekiel, putting a mark on the foreheads of the faithful (chap. 9) is followed by casting fire on the city of Jerusalem (10:1-7). In John we discern the same sequence: the sealing of the 144,000 (7:1-7) is followed by the hurling of fire on the earth (8:5).

God has heard the prayers of the saints and now responds: one catastrophe after another will come over the world.

SEVEN TRUMPETS 8:6–9:21

Seven angels will blow on trumpets, and disaster follows every trumpet blast. After Death appeared on the pale horse, a quarter of the population died (6:8). This time a third of the earth is burned up. Judgment becomes increasingly heavy. After the fourth trumpet blast, an eagle flying in midair and calling out a threefold "woe" announces the coming of the following angels. The devastation that follows the fifth and sixth trumpet blasts surpasses that of the first four. Although the punishment becomes more severe, the people do not repent.

8:6-13 FOUR TRUMPETS

The trumpet sound of the first angel unleashes very heavy weather. Lightning causes huge fires, which turn the sky blood-red. That is the "fire mixed with blood." Hail comes down as at the seventh plague in Egypt (Exod. 9:23-26). And just as the first plague in Egypt changed water into blood (Exod. 7:14-25), so here a volcanic outburst turns the sea red as blood. Sea creatures die. Ships go down. Next, rivers and springs suffer heavy damage. The star Wormwood drops down from heaven and makes the water undrinkable. It gets a bitter taste, as at Marah in the wilderness (Exod. 15:23). Orientals love sweetness, and suspect anything tasting bitter of being poisonous (Deut. 29:18; Lam. 3:19; Jer. 9:15). The bitter water (it has not been poisoned; see comments on 10:9-10) leads to the death of most of those who have drunk it. Then it is the turn of sun, moon, and stars. But the result is not Egyptian darkness, when no one could move or see anything for three days (Exod. 10:21-23). Here the intensity of the light is diminished by a third—an unusual event that filled people with fearful premonitions. At the height of it an eagle flying in midair calls out a threefold "woe" over the inhabitants of the earth.

These four disasters form a unit. The effects of the trumpet sounds of the fifth and sixth angels are described more fully. For that reason we shall deal with the fifth and sixth trumpets separately.

9:1-12 THE FIFTH TRUMPET

The first "woe" begins at the sound of the fifth trumpet. John sees a star, which has fallen from the sky, lying on earth. To it God gave the key to the shaft of the Abyss, the abode of evil spirits (Luke 8:31). When it is opened, smoke rises up as if from a crater, like that which filled the sky at the destruction of Sodom and Gomorrah (Gen. 19:28). How a star manages to unlock a door is a riddle to the intellect, but no problem in a vision.

Along with the smoke comes a special kind of locust. Ordinary locusts eat every green leaf in sight in the shortest possible time. Just think of the eighth plague in Egypt (Exod. 10:1-20). But that is precisely what these locusts did not do. They also looked very different. They were centaurs: above the waist they looked human; the rest was like a horse. They were "armed for war" (Ezek. 38:4). On their heads they wore something like a wreath of gold; they had manes like the long hair of a woman; their teeth were like lions' teeth; their chests were covered with a harness; their wings made a noise like a chariot rushing into battle; their tails had stings in them like scorpions. A sting is not deadly, but very painful. The pain, called forth by the angel with the fifth trumpet, lasted five months, as long as the Deluge (Gen. 7:24). The people whose foreheads were marked (7:3) were spared the torment—at God's command.

Ordinary locusts have no king (Prov. 30:27), but these do. He has a Hebrew name: Abaddon. Because almost no one knew Hebrew it served admirably as a code-language. It is conceivable, therefore, that a later scribe added the Greek translation "Apollyon" and so gave the solution to this riddle. Abaddon occurs in the Old Testament as "destruction" (Job 31:12) and as a place of destruction, "the abode of the dead" (Job 26:6; 28:22; Ps. 88:11; Prov. 15:11). The translator, taking Abaddon as an "abstractum pro concreto," reproduced it as Apollyon, "the Destroyer." (In the case of another Hebrew name, "Armageddon" [16:6], the Greek translation is missing, presumably because the copyist did not know its meaning.)

The material for this vision derives from an ancient Babylonian notion of a scorpion-centaur, originating out of the union of two signs of the zodiac that occur together: the archer and the scorpion.

9:13-21 THE SIXTH TRUMPET

The fifth trumpet ushered in the first "woe." Although not expressly stated, the second "woe" begins at the sixth trumpet blast. (This follows from the statement made in 8:13.) At the sound of the sixth trumpet, a voice issues from the golden altar with the four horns that is in heaven. Four angels stand ready at the Euphrates River, the eastern boundary (Gen. 15:18; Deut. 1:7; Josh. 1:4). They are bound and unable to move, but will be released at the time precisely fixed by God. That moment has come when the voice commands the angel with the trumpet to release their bonds. Then an army of 200 million mounted troops sets out to attack the human race, killing a third of it. The expected invasion of the Roman empire by the Parthians at the eastern boundary is here construed apocalyptically, as appears from the number of troops alone. If John had not heard the number he would not have known it. It agrees with the number of troops accompanying the Lord God (Ps. 68:17). The mounted troops are anti-God.

The riders had breastplates red as fire, blue as sapphire, and yellow as sulphur. The horses' heads were lions' heads, and from their mouths came fire, smoke, and sulphur. But the real venom is in their tails, which end as snakes whose bite is deadly.

In spite of all this the people who escaped did not repent. They continued to worship idols that were blind and deaf and did not move (Pss. 115:4ff.; 135:15ff.), and to practice their decadent morality. Sexual immorality, idolatry, and magical arts were the sins of Jezebel (2 Kings 9:22). Murder, magical arts, sexual immorality, and thefts were practiced daily. The word "pharmacies" in the [Gr.] text had the ugly meaning of "mixing poisons." All this is bound to boomerang. The first "woe" is past; the second is in progress; the third "woe" is coming with the seventh trumpet (11:14).

The idea that idolatry and moral decadence go hand in hand is Jewish (Rom. 1:22-32). In fairness it must be said that not all paganism has led to a decline in morality; there have been pagan cultures of high standing.

THE ANGEL WITH THE LITTLE
SCROLL 10:1-11

Just as there was a pause between the breaking of the sixth seal with its consequent judgment and the opening of the seventh seal, so there is a similar delay following the sixth trumpet blast and the horrors it releases, and before the seventh (11:15). The meaning of this intermezzo is twofold. First, there is the express assurance that at the seventh blast of the trumpet the plan of God will be carried out without delay. Second, in the interval John is instructed to make prophetic pronouncements concerning many nations, peoples, languages, and kings. To that end he has to eat a little scroll, which will be sweet as honey in his mouth but have a bitter aftertaste.

Whereas so far John was in heaven (4:1), he is now on earth again. He sees a mighty angel coming down, robed in a cloud: a striking spectacle against the clear blue sky of the Orient. Around his head is a halo that reflects the throne of God, also surrounded by a halo (4:3). His face was as radiant as the sun—another sign that he is a messenger from heaven. His legs were like columns of fire. This has some resemblance to Jesus, who appeared to John on Patmos (1:15). In his hand he has a small, open scroll, in contrast to the book that is sealed with seven seals and is in the hand of God (5:1). This angel is not the one who asked with a loud voice who was worthy to open the scroll (5:2). It is an angel of enormous proportions: with one leg he stood on the sea and with the other on the land. He has the volume of a roaring lion (Amos 3:8). The seven thunders who answer with a roar are the plural voice of the Lord God (Ps. 29). John is about to write down what the thunders have said, but instead he is instructed to seal it up, to keep it secret (Dan. 12:4, 9).

The angel swore by the Creator that at the blowing of the seventh trumpet the plan of God will be executed without delay (for the prophetic perfect, see the Introduction). It is a secret plan, revealed only to the prophets, dealing with the things that must happen (1:1). A summary of God's program is disclosed in the song of praise, which follows the blast of the seventh trumpet (11:15-18).

The same voice that called on John to keep the things he heard a secret (10:4) now commands him to go to the mighty angel with the little scroll open in his hand and to say, Give me that small scroll. John gets it and is told to eat it. It tastes sweet as honey in his mouth but it is bitter in his intestines. It sits like a stone in his stomach and causes cramps and other disturbances. This indicates that the message he must bring is not easy to digest. Prophesying is something that costs a prophet pain and effort. Ezekiel, after eating a scroll that tasted sweet in his mouth (Ezek. 2:9–3:3), went away with bitterness (3:14).

After eating the small scroll John is told: You must again prophesy about many nations, peoples, languages, and kings. This sentence contains three problems:

1. Who are "they" [see Gr. text] who say this to John? We will never know, for it is left indefinite. That often happens in apocalyptic literature; another instance, for example, is 12:6.

2. What "they" say is a quotation from the Old Testament. But where is it to be found? The first part, "You must prophesy . . . ," is quoted from Jeremiah (25:30; LXX 32:30). The same chapter offers a long list of the many peoples and princes concerning whom Jeremiah must prophesy (25:15-29). The Septuagint has for a heading over this pericope: "All that Jeremiah prophesied concerning all the nations" (LXX 32:15). John summarizes the list thus: ". . . prophesy again about many peoples, nations, languages, and kings."

3. What is the meaning of the word *again*? Usually it is said that John is told a second time to prophesy concerning many nations. In this connection there is mention of a second "call." But that interpretation is burdened by a number of serious problems:

   a) Up till now John has not made any prophetic utterances concerning many nations. How then can he be asked to do it again?
   b) If this is a second "vision of call," it is an anticlimax, as the first call came from Jesus himself (1:9-20), while this time it is from an angel (chap. 10).
   c) Prophets are called only once (Isa. 6; Jer. 1; Ezek. 1–3). Although Luke tells the story of Paul's calling to be an apostle three times (Acts 9:1-19; 22:6-16; 26:12-18), Paul, too, was called only once.

For these reasons, in my opinion, the word "again" needs to be interpreted differently. Old Testament prophets have prophesied concerning many nations and princes (Isa. 13–23; Jer. 46–51; Ezek. 25–32; Amos 1 and 2). Now, again, prophecy concerning the nations is needed. And this task will fall to John, who will do so for the first time. This is a difficult and troublesome assignment; hence that small scroll. If it had simply been bitter, he might not have swallowed it. For that reason the outside of it tastes sweet: heaven sweetens the task of preaching!

The question needs to be raised whether John, like the Old Testament prophets, in fact prophesied concerning many nations referred to by name. Apart from Babylon, John refers only to God and Magog (20:8). It is true that the whole world has gone out to battle against the church, and will pay the price. The reverse side is the promise that the nations will come to the New Jerusalem and that kings will bring their presents (21:24-26). Indeed, all nations will worship the Lord God (15:4).

TWO WITNESSES 11:1-14

After the interval in which the angel holding the small scroll appears (chap. 10), one might imagine that now the blowing of the seventh trumpet, the third "woe," and thus the final end, will follow. After all, there was to be no more delay (10:6). But John, who was instructed to make prophetic statements concerning the nations, knows that the prophets have not spared Israel, Judah, or their kings. Hard things will, therefore, have to be said concerning the Jews, who expect a new temple in the messianic era. Now John prophesies two things: (1) this future temple will suffer the same fate the old temple did in the year A.D. 70; and (2) at the construction of this new temple in the future, Zechariah's vision concerning the temple after the exile will repeat itself (Zech. 4). John therefore remains in line with Jesus' prophecy that the end will start with the destruction of the temple (Matt. 24:1ff.; Mark 13:1ff.; Luke 21:5ff.).

The key to understanding this obscure section is the expectation of the Jews that in the messianic age Jerusalem will again have a splendid temple. John does not share this belief. The New Jerusalem is a city without a temple (21:22). But he ties in with the Jewish notion of the rebuilding of the temple to show that the new temple will not at all create a new people. That, then, is John's prophetic evaluation of the Jews; it was not mild to begin with (2:9; 3:9), but this prophecy takes the prize.

It begins with the drawing and the blueprint of the temple to be erected—quite in the manner of Ezekiel 40–42. With the aid of a measuring rod, John plots the dimensions of the future temple, its altar, and the courts, where priests, men, and women will come to worship. Only the outer court has to be excluded from the building plans. That is given to the Gentiles: it is the area where heathens may set foot and as such it is not sacred territory.

But there is still another way the holy city will experience the "trampling" of the Gentiles! They will "trample" on Jerusalem and terrorize its inhabitants. To them nothing is sacred. That is something already written down in the Old Testament (Isa. 63:18; Dan. 8:13; Zech. 12:3 [LXX]). Luke, the evangelist, applies the words to the occupation of Palestine, the siege and conquest of Jerusalem in the years A.D. 66–70. Those are the times of the Gentiles, the time allotted by God to the Gentiles (Luke 21:24). John, who is writing some decades after the fall of Jerusalem, uses the same texts for the time of tyrannization that is coming and will last three and a half years. The same period can be described as forty-two months or 1,260 days (see the general Introduction).

In addition to the texts concerning the trampling down of Jerusalem, John also refers back to the history of the Jews who were faced with the heavy task of rebuilding the city and the temple. One can read about these difficulties in Ezra and Nehemiah. And when there is some thought of resisting by force the opposition of Sanballat and his colleagues (Neh. 4:7), the prophet Zechariah has a vision: "not by force or by might but by my Spirit." He sees a lampstand holding seven lamps, whose oil is supplied by two olive trees, one to the left and one to the right. These olive trees are the two anointed ones who stand before the Lord of the whole earth: the high priest Joshua and the political leader Zerubbabel (Zech. 4).

Of this vision John offers his own exegesis. He changes the one lampstand into two. And the two olive trees are Elijah and Moses, the forerunners of the Messiah. The prophet Elijah was to come back before the great and terrible Day of the Lord (Mal. 4:5). And God had promised earlier that he would raise up a prophet of the stature of Moses (Deut. 18:15, 18). It is these two whom Christ will send to the earth to function as his witnesses in that three-and-a-half-year period of terrorization. As their clothing symbolizes (v. 3), they are preachers of repentance. They have been given enormous power. If they so decide, not a drop of rain will fall in that time period (1 Kings 17:1; Luke 4:25; James 5:17); and not only the first Egyptian plague by which water was changed into blood (Exod. 7:19) but also the remaining nine are repeated. For three and a half years they are inviolable. All violent resistance is struck down by fire coming from their mouths (Num. 16:35; 2 Sam. 22:9; Isa. 11:4).

But after three and a half years their inviolability will be lifted. The beast out of the abyss appears on the scene. John is here seeing the fourth beast, which made war against the saints and conquered them (Dan. 7:7, 21). The beast, the anti-God power, kills the two witnesses and leaves their corpses unburied—the grossest insult—on the street of the great city. By this phrase John means Jerusalem, but he uses that name only for the New Jerusalem. The old Jerusalem he describes as "the great city," a designation he reserves otherwise for Babylon/Rome (17:18; 18:10, 16, 18, 19, 21). Let the reader take note of it!

Isaiah once called Jerusalem Sodom (1:10) and Ezekiel called it the sister of Sodom (Ezek. 16:48). One can hardly utter a more severe judgment. John adds to this designation the name of Egypt, the land of the "hardened" Pharaoh (Exod. 4:21, etc.). Jerusalem is the city where Jesus is crucified. And the city offers proof that it deserves to be called Sodom by celebrating the death of the two witnesses to Christ. If anyone wanted to bury them, they put a stop to it. Their hatred of Jesus is so strong that they begrudge his witnesses the privilege of burial. They are happy to be rid of them and they show it by sending each other gifts, as at the feast of Purim (Esther 9:22). Pilgrims from all parts of the world rejoice over this death. Since Golgotha nothing has changed in the attitude of the Jews.

After these three and a half days of open gloating—a period corresponding to three and a half years of witness—God causes the breath of life to enter the dead (Ezek. 37:5) and makes them stand on their feet (Ezek. 37:10). Terror now strikes the people. They hear the voice of God commanding the two witnesses to "come up." Their enemies (!) watch it happen. A heavy earthquake follows (Ezek. 38:19-20). Ten percent of the houses in Jerusalem collapse and 7,000 people die. The survivors are terrified and "give glory to God." That does not mean they now begin to praise God, however; that would be very strange in such a situation. The expression "to give glory to God" should remind us of Joshua's summons to Achan: "Give glory to the Lord, the God of Israel, and confess to him. Tell me what you have done . . ." (Josh. 7:19). Achan confesses everything, and the people stone him and all his possessions. In terror the people in Jerusalem list their sins. But that hardly adds up to conversions. This lack of repentance was twice mentioned after the blast of the sixth trumpet (9:20-21). Apparently, that is characteristic for the second "woe." That, now, is past. When the seventh angel blows his trumpet the third "woe" will begin.

THE SEVENTH TRUMPET 11:15-19

Six angels have sounded their trumpets (chaps. 8 and 9). Next, John is instructed to prophesy concerning the nations (chap. 10). But first he prophesied that the Jews would be punished because they gloated over the death of the two witnesses to Christ (11:1-14). Now comes the seventh trumpet blast.

The seventh trumpet sounds the arrival of the end. The third "woe" is about to begin. Anticipating the things "that must soon take place" (1:1, 19; 4:1), voices in heaven celebrate God's victory over his enemies as though the battle had already been won. The words have been chosen from Psalm 2: "the Lord and his Anointed One" (v. 2), "the wrath of God" (vv. 5, 12). God has put an end to the revolution against his authority. He demonstrated his power, proving who really was king.

The moment for the resurrection from the dead and the final judgment has, therefore, come. To be rewarded are the prophets, "the saints of the Most High" (Dan. 7:21, 22, 25, 27), and those, young or old, who reverence the name of the Lord (Ps. 115:13). That includes three categories of people: preachers of the Word, church members, and people who, without joining the church, reverence the Lord God. That final element will also count with the Judge. And that applies to both young and old. On the last day there will also be a settling of accounts with those who have brought destruction on the earth, that is, on the inhabitants of the earth (cf. 13:2, 12; 14:3; 19:2).

Thus the twenty-four elders thank God that he has begun to reign. They no longer call out to him as he who is, was, and who is to come (1:8; 4:8), but only he "who is and who was" (11:16). He *has* come.

In response to the songs of praise God opens his temple in heaven. The ark of the covenant becomes visible. Scholars have held various views with regard to the ark. Some have thought of the Jewish legend that the ark which Jeremiah had hidden in a cleft of a rock would reappear in the messianic era (2 Macc. 2:4-8). But in Revelation 11:19 the reference is not to an earthly ark. Nor is it relevant to bring up the theological consideration that access to God has been free ever since the curtain in front of the holy of holies split (Matt. 27:51; Mark 15:38; Luke 23:45). This view, which is correct in itself, is also bound up with the temple on earth. But 11:19 has no reference to it. In this passage the ark is the sign of the presence of God. He shows that he is present as the Holy One. Natural phenomena awesomely accentuate his presence (4:5; 8:5; 16:18). The fact that the reference is to the holiness of God is evident from the parallel (15:5-8), where the tabernacle is opened after the victory song has been sung and the seven angels, having the seven bowls of the wrath of God, pour out his anger over the earth.

THE WOMAN AND THE DRAGON 12:1-17

After the seventh trumpet blast there is singing in heaven, as it anticipates the victory of God over the nations that rebel against the Lord and his Anointed. The third "woe" is about to take place (11:14). It occurs—without being called by that name—when the bowls filled with wrath are emptied (chap. 16). But first some other matters are cleared up. In 11:7 there was reference to the beast out of the Abyss. Because the devil is behind the beast, John has to give further detail on that issue, and so returns to it in chapter 13. To that end he offers us the vision of the Woman and the Dragon (chap. 12). The primeval Dragon threatens the prospective mother of the Messiah in order to devour her child. By that action the Satan loses his place in heaven. Michael and his angels cast the Satan and his angels out of heaven upon the earth. There he vents his fury on Christians. From now on the earth and the sea are the arena of his activities. The cry: "Woe to the earth and the sea" (12:12) keeps alive the memory of the coming of the third "woe."

12:1-6 THE WOMAN AND THE DRAGON

One could regard the twelfth chapter of Revelation as John's commentary on the words addressed to the serpent in Paradise: "I will put enmity between you and the woman, and between your seed and her seed; he shall bruise your head and you shall bruise his heel" (Gen. 3:15). Eve, the mother of all living (Gen. 3:20), and her children will have to be on their guard against the serpent. Wherever human beings walk they will have to watch out against the poisonous teeth of this devious enemy, which loves to attack from behind. But one of Eve's descendants will kill the old serpent, the devil, the Satan (12:9) by crushing the beast's head.

John lets the stars tell this story—a common practice at that time and in that world. The ancient Babylonians called the stars the writing of the gods. What the gods have to say to people they write in the stars. So the book uses the stars to illustrate the word of the Lord God.

John sees the constellation Virgo light up sharply in the sky. The sun is her robe. By that fact she is clearly aligned with God, who covers himself with light as with a garment (Ps. 104:2). While God has the earth as his footstool (Isa. 66:1), the Woman has the moon. There is something royal in the way her head is crowned with twelve stars. She is expecting a baby, which may come at any time.

Then another sign appears in heaven: the Dragon. This constellation extends along the Milky Way over four signs of the zodiac: the Balance, the Virgin, the Lion, and the Crab. In John's vision the Dragon is bright red, and a fire glows in its body. It has seven heads, with a crown on each. In his own way the Dragon is a king. His ten horns suggest his great power.

The Dragon places itself in front of the Woman to devour her child the moment it is born. With its tail it sweeps a third of the stars out of the sky. It knows that the child the Woman will bear is the Messiah, the Shepherd-king who will attack the enemies of his flock with an iron rod (Ps. 2:9; Rev. 2:27; 19:15). Therefore the Dragon immediately tries to render the little boy harmless. But the child is snatched up to God and to his throne and made safe. The Woman escapes his wrath and flees to the wilderness, where she is taken care of for 1,260 days. It is entirely in keeping with apocalyptic literature that we are not told who snatches up the child or who takes care of the Woman.

It is plain who is meant by the Dragon, though. He is pictured with the symbolism of the fourth beast from the Book of Daniel. It also had ten horns (Dan. 7:7, 24). That beast was Antiochus Epiphanes IV, the representative of anti-God powers in the Maccabean war. He took stars out of the sky and trampled them (Dan. 8:10); he taunted the God of Israel by violating his temple (Dan. 8:11). In John's days this anti-Christian power is embodied in the Roman empire, which persecuted Christians. The Dragon with its ten horns and seven heads—a crown on every one of them—returns in the Beast with the ten crowned horns and seven heads bearing blasphemous names (13:1), and in the great harlot Rome who is seated on the scarlet beast bearing blasphemous names, having ten horns and seven heads (17:3).

The Woman is the mother of the Messiah. It is somewhat natural to think of Mary here, but the image of the Woman is not in harmony with the Mary of the gospels. In the gospels there is no Mary clothed with the sun, having the moon under her feet as a footstool and a crown of twelve stars. Nor is there a separation between mother and child there, the child being snatched up to heaven and the woman escaping to the desert.

The 1,260 days refer to the period of the messianic woes (11:2-3), which precede the kingdom of God. It is the time of the oppression. In that case, the Woman could be the church pressed hard by the Dragon. But the church did not bring forth the Messiah! Quite the reverse is true: the church owes its existence to the Messiah.

Is the Woman Eve, perhaps? The term "her offspring" (12:17) is taken directly from Genesis 3:15. The Dragon makes war against Eve's descendants, that is, against Christians, not humankind in general. Still, it seems best to me to view "the Woman and the Dragon" as a visionary explanation of the struggle between the woman, her children, and the dragon. Since the devil could not eliminate her son, the Messiah who would crush the serpent's head, his fury now erupts against the Woman. But because she also escapes his wrath, he attacks her offspring, the Christ-believers. This is how the persecution of Christians by the Roman empire is written in the stars. Stars by themselves do not say anything. They only begin to speak when the Spirit actualizes the Word. Then the constellations serve to illustrate Holy Scripture.

12:7-12 MICHAEL AND THE DRAGON

War in heaven! We can hardly conceive of it, any more than the presence of fallen angels in heaven; and still less the presence of the devil there. Earth is the scene of war and rumors of war. Earth is where apostasy takes place, the sphere of the devil's labor.

But there are chapters in the Old Testament in which Satan is not yet the "devil." In the Book of Job, Satan appears before God in heaven. There Satan is a servant of God who regularly reports on human behavior. God makes a wager with Satan, as it were, concerning the piety of Job (chaps. 1 and 2). In another account, the prophet Zechariah sees a "vision" in which Joshua the high priest stands in front of the Angel of the Lord. Satan submits a protest: as a result of the exile Joshua has become unclean and is therefore unfit for high office. Satan points a finger at the filthy clothes of Joshua, a fact that cannot be denied. At last, all the Angel of the Lord can do is dismiss the devil with a curse (Zech. 3:1-3).

Satan is not yet the great Deceiver who delights in drawing people away from God. That comes later, as for instance in more recent books like Chronicles where Satan incites David to sin (1 Chron. 21:1). In the New Testament, Satan is the arch-foe of God. But Jesus still knows of the time Satan resided in heaven; witness his statement, "I saw Satan fall like lightning from heaven" (Luke 10:18). This is reminiscent of Isaiah, who compared the king of Babylon with Lucifer: "How you are fallen from heaven, O Day Star, son of Dawn! How you are cut down to the ground, you who laid the nations low!" (Isa. 14:12). Satan has become an apostate angel and has succeeded in getting other angels to join him (Jude 6). They will not escape their punishment; they are destined for the fire of hell (Matt. 25:41). For that purpose they are kept in "gloomy dungeons" (2 Pet. 2:4).

When the Dragon wants to lay violent hands on the Messiah the measure is full. Michael and his angels cannot tolerate it. It is their mandate to hurl the Dragon and his angels from heaven, and they succeed, although after a hard battle. Thus the Dragon and his henchmen are hurled down to earth: the persistent and fanatic prosecutor who laid his indictments against Christians before God day and night is now expelled. This is cause for joy in heaven but an occasion of deep anxiety for the earth and the sea. The Dragon has not yet been destroyed. He will use to the utmost the short time still left him to avenge the defeat he has suffered. He is furious. Like a roaring lion he will go in search of whomever he can devour (1 Pet. 5:8).

The serpent in Paradise deceived Eve. The devil who deceives the whole world will have no success with believers, however. They have overcome him by the blood of the Lamb. Their sin has been atoned for on the cross—by that conviction they stand and to it they will continue to witness even if they have to pay for it with their lives. They did not overvalue their lives—they did not regard it as the greatest good. "To love" in Scripture often means to put something or someone in first place. "To hate," then, is to put something or someone in second, third, or an even lesser place. Loving and hating have to do with priorities. In that light we must read texts like Matthew 6:24; Luke 16:13 and Matthew 10:37; Luke 14:26 and Romans 9:13.

It is only in the sequel that we learn what is implied in the devil's leading the whole world astray. It is the temptation that proceeds from emperor-worship (13:14). This also explains what "overcoming" means (12:11); it is noncooperation with the worship of the beast and his image.

12:13-17 THE DRAGON AND THE WOMAN

As soon as the Dragon has recovered from the experience of crashing down to earth, he begins to pursue the Woman, who had fled to the desert. How she accomplished this is now revealed: she was given the eagle's ability to fly—the capacity of a great bird "with powerful wings, long feathers and full plumage of varied colors" (Ezek. 17:3, 7). And just as the Lord God carried Israel on eagle's wings out of Egypt into the desert (Exod. 19:4) and kept his people alive with manna from heaven and water from a rock, so the Woman flies to the desert. There she is taken care of "a time, times, and half a time." This time, indication of which we also find in Daniel, equals three and a half years (Dan. 7:25; 12:7), which is forty-two months (11:2) or 1,260 days (11:3; 12:6).

The Woman is now outside the Dragon's reach. Only one means of destroying her life remains to him. From his mouth he spews forth a stream of water like a river with the idea of overtaking the fleeing Woman and causing her death by drowning. The Dragon occurs elsewhere in the Old Testament as a sea monster. God himself will kill the Leviathan (Isa. 27:1); he has crushed the heads of Leviathan (Ps. 74:14); he cut Rahab to pieces and pierced the sea monster through (Isa. 51:9); he crushed Rahab (Ps. 89:10). Mythology itself also offers examples of the battle against the monsters that live in the sea.

The earth helps the Woman; it "opened its mouth and swallowed the river"—phrasing which is reminiscent of Numbers 16:30, 32. With the Woman out of reach the Dragon now directs his fury against her other children. The one child is the Christ; the others are the Christians. They obey God's commandments and hold to the testimony of Jesus (1:2, 9; 6:9; 19:10).

In his rage the Dragon went in the direction of the sea and remained standing on the shore. The reading "And I stood on the shore of the sea" (13:1, KJV) is not supported by the earliest manuscripts. It is not John but the Dragon who stands on the shore of the sea and calls the beast out of the sea to make war against the saints (13:7).

TWO BEASTS 13:1-18

After he describes the Dragon, John witnesses the two instruments he uses: two beasts. The first emerges from the sea and represents the Roman empire; the other comes up out of a cleft in the earth and represents the priestcraft of the state temples. The Dragon transfers his power to the first beast, which in turn uses the second beast to seduce people into worshiping the emperor as divine. These three form a hierarchy: the Dragon, the Beast, and the beast. (To tell them apart we shall print the first with a capital B and the second with a lower case b.) The Beast is further described with the number 666; the beast is later characterized as a false prophet (16:13; 19:20; 20:10). In Paul's letters the state is the servant of God (Rom. 13:4); in John it is the devil's lackey.

13:1-10 THE BEAST OUT OF THE SEA

The beast that came up out of the underworld began the attack against the two witnesses, overpowered them, and killed them (11:7). That is all we know so far about that beast. The case is different with the Beast out of the sea, which is pictured in images from the Book of Daniel. Daniel saw four beasts coming out of the sea: the first looked like a lion, the second resembled a bear, the third a leopard, and the fourth was a dreadful monster with ten horns (Dan. 7:1-8). John merges these four into one Beast having ten horns, each with a crown, and seven heads, each of them bearing a blasphemous name. This Beast is the Roman Empire and the heads are the emperors who had themselves worshiped as gods. Domitian was addressed as "our Lord and God"—a practice against which the twenty-four elders protested (4:11).

The Beast comes up out of the sea. It was thought in those days that the sea was the nursery of anti-God powers. For that reason there will be a new heaven and a new earth but no sea (21:1). Thus the chaos where monsters are bred will have disappeared. From the Dragon the Beast receives his power, throne, and authority. As a result the Roman empire is no longer a servant of God (Rom. 13:1-7) but a slave of the devil. Rome underwent a serious crisis when Nero committed suicide in A.D. 68, ending the "divine" dynasty of the Julians. An interim government under Galba, Otho, and Vitellius (A.D. 68-69) followed. A new generation—the Flavians—came on the scene with Vespasian (A.D. 69-79), and the empire recovered. This is "the recovery from the deadly wound" referred to in 13:14. (This matter will surface again in chapter 17.) John characterizes that "resurrection" as a caricature of the

Lamb that was slain but is standing (5:6): it was as though it had been slain but it survived the deadly blow and recovered.

The world had not believed this was still possible. The whole world, that is, all people on earth, are astonished and follow the Beast. Gratefully they worship the Dragon because he has enthroned the Beast. On their knees they offer the Beast an ovation with choral chants: Who is like the Beast? In Christian ears that sounds like an imitation of what was said of the God of Israel: "Who is a God like you?" (Mic. 7:18); "Who among the gods is like you, O Lord?" (Exod. 15:11). (See also Isa. 40:25; 44:7; 46:5; Pss. 89:8; 113:5.) The answer to the question, "Who can successfully make war against the Beast?" is, of course, no one.

Similar sentiments can be heard in the boasting and blasphemies of the Beast. And that, again, is in keeping with the character of the fourth monster in the Book of Daniel (Dan. 7:8, 20, 25; 11:36). This blasphemy of God and his name, of heaven and its inhabitants, takes place by God's permission, as also the war that is waged (successfully) on the saints (Dan. 7:21), that is, the persecution of Christians. Nor was the fact that the Roman empire became a world power something that happened outside the will of God. The Dragon had given authority to the Beast; but it is God who determines its beginning and end. After forty-two months it is all over. This is a time limit we have encountered before (11:2): forty-two months equals 1,260 days (11:3; 12:6), which equals three and a half years (12:14).

John prophesies that the entire world will worship the Beast, who is the emperor, as representative of the empire. Everyone whose name is not written in the book of life will take part in this worship. From the beginning of creation the names of those who will inherit eternal life (3:5) have been written down in the book, which is in the custody of the Lamb that was slain. Incidentally, the expression "from the creation of the world" qualifies the recording of the names, not the slaying of the Lamb, as may be evident from 17:8, where the same terminology is used [cf. RSV; the NIV offers this possibility in a footnote on 13:8].

For the believers, that book of life is a great comfort. They are facing hard times—even though their duration has been determined by God. John calls special attention to an utterance of the prophet Jeremiah: those destined for captivity will go into captivity; those destined for the sword will be killed by the sword. To read this accurately, however, one needs good eyes and sharp ears. The text of Revelation has not been transmitted whole and undamaged. Jeremiah's succinct formulation ("those destined for death, to death; those for the sword, to the sword; those for starvation, to starvation; those for captivity, to captivity"; Jer. 15:2, NIV) has occasioned misunderstanding. With Jesus' words ("all who draw the sword will die by the sword") in their minds and hearts, the interpreters of Jeremiah read the prophet as saying that if someone killed with the sword that person would himself be killed with the sword. This, in turn, led to the result that the verse was interpreted to say that if anyone led another into captivity, he himself will be led captive. That, then, is a warning addressed to the Roman overlords: whatever you do to Christians will be done to you; at the same time it served as an admonition to Christians not to defend themselves with weapons of violence. But none of this fits the context. The author's concern is not with the church's arsenal of weapons; his concern is over the church's faith and endurance. The object is to persevere and to remain faithful (cf. Matt. 24:13; Mark 13:13).

13:11-18 THE BEAST OUT OF THE EARTH

The Beast came up out of the sea; the beast comes out of the earth. It had hidden in one of the clefts in the rocks that are so plentiful on the earth, in which robbers often hid to attack lonely travelers (Luke 10:30). A number of circumstances indicate that the Beast is the beast's superior:

1. The Beast had ten horns, each with a crown, and seven heads (13:1). The beast has only two horns, small as the horns of a lamb. Still, it needs to be watched: it speaks like the ancient serpent in Paradise, which persuaded Eve to disobey the commandment of God. It is a false prophet in sheep's clothing (Matt. 7:15) and therefore all the more dangerous.

2. The Beast rules over the beast. The Dragon had given his authority to the Beast (13:2); the Beast, in turn, gives his authority to the beast. But the Beast continues to watch carefully to see whether the beast uses that power correctly (13:12, 14).

3. The beast serves the greater glory of the Beast. The

mandate of the beast is to see to it that people will worship the Beast. The Beast is the Roman empire that, after the death of Nero and following a deep crisis, recovered. It's recovery must have made a profound impression on John, as he mentions it three times in the same chapter (13:3, 12, 14; cf. also 17:8). It is the job of the beast to exploit this unexpected event; it must persuade people to give the emperor the glory due to God alone.

4. The goal of the Beast is military: to wage war against the saints and to conquer them (13:4, 7). The beast has a prophetic task: to seduce people to offer worship to the goddess Roma. By means of miracles it convinces the world of its prophetic office, and soon people are ready to respond favorably to its call and to make an image of the Beast. For that reason John calls the beast a false prophet (16:13; 19:20; 20:10). One recalls that Jesus had already warned people that false prophets would arise and do great signs and wonders (Matt. 24:24; Mark 13:22).

Just who or what does the beast represent? It represents the priests of the state temples where the statue of the divine emperor ("divus Augustus") was put and on whose altar sacrifices were offered. It was well known that the priests performed a variety of stunts and tricks to throw dust into the eyes of a superstitious people. They imitated the sounds of a thunderstorm. A flash of light was "fire from heaven" (13:13) and the sound of a thunderclap the voice of the god. And what the god said came out of the mouth of the priest who had crept into the hollow statue. The world wants to be deceived; therefore let it be deceived ("Mundus vult decipi, ergo decipiatur"). John was familiar with such practices. The image "got the spirit" and therefore spoke (13:15).

And what did the spirit of the image of the Beast say? It said that everyone who did not kneel before the image should receive the death penalty. John must have had in mind the story of Nebuchadnezzar, who had an image made and who then ordered that anyone who did not cast himself down on the ground would be thrown into the fire of a super-heated furnace (Dan. 3:1-7). That threat did not fail to have effect, neither then nor now. Everyone took part in the emperor cult. Age, position, and possessions no longer mattered. The false prophet, using fear as a means of pressure, triumphed on the entire front.

And just as masters branded slaves as proof of ownership in case they ran away, so priests placed a mark on the right hand or forehead of those who had fulfilled their religious obligations with respect to the divine emperor. In the sacred halls of the state one received the sacred hallmark of the state. And that, then, was the equivalent of the sealing of the saints (7:2-8).

For those Christians who refused this kind of loyalty to the emperor the consequences were very serious. Buying and selling were tied in with the possession of the mark of the Beast. A person lacking this stamp could not do business in the marketplace. Such a person could not earn money or buy provisions for his or her own support and would therefore become a pauper or die of starvation.

That mark itself consisted of the name of the Beast or the numerical value of the letters of his name.* To the Hebrews, letters also served as numbers: thus A=1; B=2; C=3; D=4, etc. So the girl's name ADA had the numerical value of 1 plus 4 plus 1, which equals 6. In that manner every name could be expressed in numbers. The reverse was a guessing game. One offered a number and asked for a name. To pursue this example: one gave the number 6, and asked "what is the name?" That can be ADA. But it also can be AAD, for 1 plus 1 plus 4 equals 6. Now tell us the name of the person whose number is 666. Further, one could make the guessing game even more complicated by moving the numbers up one letter or more. This was not unusual in devising codes. ADA then became BEB, CFC, DGD, etc. An experienced puzzler could test his or her skills on the riddle, a genuine brainteaser. Therefore, the number of solutions for the number 666 is legion.

One must start with the assumption that the number of the Beast is the number of a man (13:18). Under the circumstances, this could only be one man—the emperor of the Roman empire. It stands to reason that one should think of Domitian, under whose rule the book of Revelation was written. That, indeed, is the case. But to do so we need to transcribe the words "Emperor Domitian" into Hebrew and move each letter by eighteen numbers. But to explain the whole

*Verse 18 in the author's translation reads: "Here cleverness will show. Whoever has insight [into numerical riddles] must figure out the number of the Beast, because the number stands for a man's name. Its number is 666."—*Trans.*

issue would take us too far afield. I have elsewhere defended the thesis that the original reading was not 666 but 616. The reason for the change is that people did not know what to do with the number 616 and therefore substituted the number 666, which gives the precise numerical value of the Hebrew translation of the Greek word for Beast. But that cannot be correct: John has expressly told us that it is the number of a human being.

THE LAMB AND THE 144,000 14:1-5

The seventh angel had already sounded the last trumpet (11:15). In heaven God's final victory has already been celebrated (11:15-18). After that, attention is fixed on the big three: the Dragon, the Beast, and the beast, the real triumvirate running the Roman empire. Now the hour of judgment is to be proclaimed. But before this happens there is a fresh focus on the 144,000. In 7:1-8 we learned they were being sealed. Now we learn who they are.

The Beast managed to get the priests to mark all persons without distinction with the sign of the Beast (13:16). But not everyone actually worshiped it. It was as in the days of Daniel: the masses kneeled before the image that Nebuchadnezzar had set up, but Shadrach, Meshach, and Abednego did not fall down to the ground to worship it (Dan. 3:8-12). Similarly, the Christians refused to take part along with others in worshiping the emperor. Their refusal brought them into grave difficulties, and for that reason John now encourages them.

John sees the Lamb standing on Mount Zion, and with him are the 144,000 sealed ones who bear on their foreheads the name of the Lamb and that of his Father. This, then, is a counterpart to those who bear the brand of the Beast.

From heaven John hears an enormous flood of sound, like the sound of many waters, having the same volume as Jesus had in John's vision of his call (1:15). It boomed like a peal of thunder, with a voice like that of one of the four living beings before the throne (6:1). It sounded like the sound of harpists (5:8). To our ears that is a strange combination of sounds, but in visions more things can happen than we think possible.

And there is singing—we are not told by whom, but it is a new song that is sounded. We encountered this before

(5:9), but this time we are not told the content of the song. Only the 144,000 have heard it, and only they can learn it. That is the privilege especially granted them. The words and the melody remain secret, however.

These 144,000 have been redeemed. This is a term connected with the sacred redemptive purchase of a slave. Whenever someone paid the price of a certain slave in the temple, that slave became a free man. Out of all humankind Jesus redeemed his own by his blood (5:9; cf. 1 Cor. 6:20; Gal. 3:13; 4:5; 2 Pet. 2:1).

In the messianic age the redeemed of the Lord will come into Zion with rejoicing along the holy highway on which no impure person will put his feet (Isa. 35:8-10). John sees this in a vision. The redeemed have arrived in Zion. There is joy in heaven. And therefore there is singing! There is no impurity among these pilgrims; they are a body of picked people. As soldiers involved in a holy war they have no association with women (1 Sam. 21:4, 5; 2 Sam. 11:11). Even more strongly, they have totally abstained from marriage, not because marriage is bad but because they wanted to be able to follow the Lamb wherever he went (Matt. 8:19; Luke 9:57). To tie oneself down to wife and children would be a hindrance (1 Cor. 7:25-40). So they are virginal—a concept applied not only to girls but also to unmarried men.

There is still another respect in which they are pure. In their mouths there is no deception. In that respect, also, they have followed Jesus (1 Pet. 2:22; Isa. 53:9). Not being deceptive is one of the marks of a righteous person (Ps. 32:2; John 1:48). Not having a deceptive tongue is a feature of the age of redemption (Zeph. 3:13).

The 144,000 are the first of humankind to be redeemed for God and for the Lamb. Therefore it is their privilege to hear the song sung in heaven. Next to the innumerable throng of the blessed ones before the throne they form a separate group (7:2-8). They are the elite: the crack troops of the *militia Christi*.

THE PROCLAMATION OF JUDGMENT 14:6-20

This section is an excellent example of John's gift for composition. Three angels, each in his own way, announce the judgment that is coming. Then the Son of God appears. The fourth angel conveys to him the command of God to mow down and reap the earth like a grainfield. The sixth angel commands the fifth angel in the name of God to cut off the clusters of the vine, to gather them, and to throw them into the winepress. Six angels are involved: two times three. And the Son of Man is the central figure in the middle!

14:6-13 THREE ANGELS

Each of the three angels has a message. The first angel's assignment is to proclaim the eternal gospel. He is flying in mid-heaven so that everyone can hear him—like the cry of the eagle announcing the threefold "woe" (8:13). The "gospel" is the plan of God, which he made ages ago and which will now be realized. The final judgment is about to begin and therefore the whole world is summoned to fear God (i.e., to tremble before his holiness), to give him glory (i.e., to confess one's sin; see comments on 11:13; 16:9), and to worship him who has created all things.

The second angel anticipates the very near future with words derived from Isaiah: "Fallen, fallen is Babylon the great" (Isa. 21:9). That, then, was the Babylon of which Nebuchadnezzar was so proud (Dan. 4:30), and that made the nations drunk with its heady wine (Jer. 51:7) so that they let themselves be seduced into "prostitution," exchanging their own gods for those of Babylon. What the Old Testament attributes to Babylon, John ascribes to the Roman empire. Babylon, therefore, means Rome (cf. 1 Pet. 5:13). It is so certain that Babylon will fall that its fall can be proclaimed from the housetops as though it had already happened. (For the use of the "prophetic perfect," see the general Introduction of this book.)

From the sequel one can tell that Babylon signifies Rome. The third angel announces the penalty of emperor-worship. Everyone who has received the mark or the name of the Beast will drink the heady wine that God has prepared. As a rule wine was diluted with water to reduce its strength. Those who wanted to serve a full-bodied drink did not dilute it but added ingredients that considerably heightened the effect. The wine that God has poured into the cup of his wrath is undiluted and well spiced (for the cup of God's wrath, see Ps. 75:8; Isa. 51:17, 22; Jer. 25:15; 49:12; Lam. 4:21; Ezek. 23:31-35;

Hab. 2:16). Those who will drink of this cup are Babylon and those who have participated in the deification of the emperor.

This punishment is illustrated in still another way. Fire and brimstone, which came down as precipitation on Sodom and Gomorrah (Gen. 19:24), will function as the means of torment. This torment will take place before the eyes of the holy angels and in the presence of the Lamb. Victims will be all the more remorseful when they see the angels and the Lamb. If only we had believed!

A prophecy concerning Edom provides the material for illuminating still another side of the picture. The punishment will be eternal. Its land turns to blazing pitch, which burns night and day; its smoke will rise forever (Isa. 34:10). The smoke of the fire and the fumes of the sulfur will continue to rise without interruption. Those who bear the mark of the Beast will no longer find any rest.

The "eternal gospel" (14:6) is the fall of the Roman empire that persecuted the Christians because they refused to give to the emperor that to which only God and the Lamb are entitled. Part of that "eternal gospel" is eternal punishment. The reverse, the reward of believers, which was mentioned in 11:18 in connection with the coming judgment, is left unmentioned here. All that is said is that everything now depends on the perseverance of the saints: those who keep the commandments of God and hold to the faith in Jesus. The term "saints" is derived from Daniel (Dan. 7:18, 22, 27).

What now follows is so important that John is instructed to write it down. The dead who die in the Lord from this moment forward are congratulated. There is movement toward a climax. Oppression will grow heavier. The moment the enemy discovers that he will suffer defeat, he becomes malevolent. He will cause a maximum of misery to compensate for his losses. And Christians who die now will be spared this furious oppression. The Spirit affirms this; they are blessed indeed! And he adds a wish, that they may rest from their intense effort. They have not had an easy time. But their deeds, the deeds by which they will be judged in the final judgment, will go with them. They were prepared to give up everything for their faith.

Those who bear the mark of the Beast will have no rest—ever. The believing dead may rest until the great Day arrives, but we are not told where. The martyrs rest under the altar in heaven (6:11). Whether that is the case here is not disclosed. The Bible says little about "the intermediate state" (i.e., the state of the dead between death and resurrection). We must therefore practice modesty. R.I.P., *Requiescat In Pace*: May he or she rest in peace. This is not a magic formula to ward off vandals or demons who might violate the grave, but originally a reference to the words of a psalm: "In peace I will both lie down and sleep; for thou alone, O Lord, makest me dwell in safety" (Ps. 4:8).

14:14-16 THE SON OF MAN AND THE FOURTH ANGEL

After the three angels have spoken, the Son of Man appears with a sharp sickle in his hand. The designation "Son of Man" derives from the Book of Daniel, where someone "like a son of man" is coming with the clouds of heaven (7:13). The Hebrew word *adam* is a collective noun and refers to people (plural). To indicate that one wants to speak of a single person one refers to "the son of man," that is, a man (singular). In Daniel 7 this man represents the faithful Israel that keeps the law (Torah). In the New Testament, the Son of Man is the heavenly Judge (John 5:27-29). But since this expression was not understood in the Greco-Roman world (is not everyone the son of man?) it was translated "judge of the living and the dead" (Acts 10:42), "who is to judge the living and the dead" (2 Tim. 4:1; cf. 1 Pet. 4:5).

It seems strange to us that an angel, who is so much lower in rank, can issue commands to the Son of Man. But the fourth angel emerges directly from the heavenly sanctuary (11:19) and speaks directly in the name of God. The command is the same as that preserved in the prophecies of Joel: "Put in the sickle, for the harvest is ripe" (Joel 3:13). The earth is a grainfield. The grain is dry as cork and has to be harvested. It is past high time. The harvest is a well-known image for the final judgment (e.g., in the parable of the weeds in the field, Matt. 13:36-43). The Son of Man swings his sickle into grain that is overripe. The final judgment has begun.

14:17-20 THE FIFTH AND SIXTH ANGELS

Next, John sees the fifth angel come out of the heavenly sanctuary. He, too, has a sharp sickle in his hand, like the Son of Man (14:14-16). Then the sixth angel steps forward. He has access to the fire on the altar. It was he who provided the angel with the golden censer with incense and fire (8:3-5). He comes out of the altar, which is, as it were, his place of residence. Under that altar were the souls of the martyrs (6:9). Out of the horns of that altar came a voice (9:13). The altar even has the ability to speak (16:7). In a vision, therefore, an angel can come out of an altar. That which he has to say is the Word of God.

The sixth angel commands the fifth angel, the one with the sickle-shaped knife, to cut off the clusters of grapes. This command also occurs in the prophecies of Joel: "Go in, tread, for the wine press is full. The vats overflow, for their wickedness is great" (Joel 3:13)! The grapes are gathered, thrown into the winepress, and trampled to let the juice run down to the vats below. This process, too, is a picture of the final judgment. The grapes are thrown "into the great wine press of the wrath of God." This takes place outside the city, referring to Jerusalem. The Jews expected that the final judgment would take place in the proximity of Jerusalem. Joel points to the valley of Jehoshaphat, which is the valley of decision, for this purpose (Joel 3:2, 12, 14). Geographically, the valley does not exist. It is a symbolic name: God judges. It is the valley of an irrevocably fixed judgment of annihilation. In the fourth century A.D. it was identified with the valley of Kedron. But that valley is much too narrow for a bloody battle in which the nations are annihilated.

John sees the wine vats run over. The red juice of the grapes turns into blood and forms a river of sixteen hundred stadia [about 192 miles]. In that river of blood the war horses wade up to their bridles. In the prophecies of Isaiah God's garments are blood-stained from treading the wine press of his wrath (Isa. 63:2-3). He trampled nations in his anger, made them drunk, and caused their blood to run to the ground (Isa. 63:6). That is still a small matter (hard though it is to picture God in these terms!) compared with John's graphic depiction of the effects of God's wrath. In the apocryphal Book of Enoch we find a similar description: in the days before the last judgment sinners will murder each other from sunrise to sundown; a warhorse will wade in the blood of sinners up to his chest and a military chariot will go down in it up to its top.

Why a river of sixteen hundred stadia? Why not twelve hundred or one thousand? Those are sacred numbers, too!

Some refer to an ancient traveler's tale that tells us that the distance from Tyre to the Egyptian border is sixteen hundred stadia. And that, then, is the entire length of the promised land. In my opinion, however, there is a better solution. The starting point is the text quoted from Isaiah (63:6). God caused the blood of nations to run on the ground. For "causing to run" the Hebrew uses the same word that occurs in the name of the river Jordan, at least as far as the consonants are concerned. The meandering river Jordan, from its source to the Dead Sea, has a length of 320 kilometers. As the crow flies that is a distance of 260 kilometers. Taking an average, we arrive at 290 kilometers (pedestrians can cut off corners). One stadium is 600 Greek feet, which equals 185 meters. The equivalent of 1,600 stadia is 296 kilometers. The blood river must therefore be as great in length as the Jordan. This remains true if we use the Roman foot. One stadium is 625 Roman feet, or 192 meters; 1,600 stadia then equals 307.2 kilometers.

THE SONG OF MOSES AND THE LAMB 15:1-4

It is characteristic of Revelation that the future is anticipated in song. That happened in the song of heaven and in the response of the twenty-four elders (11:15-18). It is also the case in the song of Moses and the Lamb. This song anticipates the judgment of God, and introduces the vision of the seven angels with the bowls full of the wrath of God.

The sounding of the seventh trumpet (11:15) announced the coming of the wrath of God (11:18). Whoever worships the emperor as a god is given the wine of God's wrath to drink (14:10). The Son of Man has harvested the earth (14:14-16). The grapes have been trampled in the wine press of the wrath of God (14:20). That will be—indeed, that has now been—fulfilled (prophetic perfect; see general Introduction). Seven angels now appear with the seven last plagues. The *last* plagues! When the seven bowls have been poured out (16:1) the great city of Babylon is finished and the proud Roman empire has become history.

John hears Christians sing; they are the people who have not given the emperor that which is due only to God. By refusing to participate in the imperial cult, they have overcome the Beast, its image, and its number; that is, the emperor (for the number of his name, see my comments on 13:18).

These Christians are standing by the sea of glass, which is before the throne of God (4:6). We are now told in addition that this sea of glass was mixed with fire. Among the Romans the art of glassmaking had reached a high level of development. The artisans added red, green, blue, and yellow pseudo-gemstones to the glass as ornamentation. They were also able to produce wavy lines of color in the glass. John sees bright-colored flames in it.

The Christians by the sea have the harps of God in their hands. Those are musical instruments belonging to God and his service, the same as those with which the twenty-four elders accompanied their singing (5:8) and with which the singing in heaven is accompanied (14:2).

The victors sing the song of Moses and the Lamb. This song is a combination of a number of texts from Scripture. Three lines of it derive from the song of Moses (Exod. 15 and Deut. 32); the rest are from the prophecies of Jeremiah and the Book of Psalms. Great and marvelous are the deeds of God (Exod. 15:11); just and true are your ways (Deut. 32:4). You alone are holy (Deut. 32:4, LXX). King of the ages, who will not fear you (Jer. 10:6-7)? All the nations you have made will come and worship before you, O Lord (Ps. 86:9).

This is clearly a song in honor of God. How can it simultaneously be a song of the Lamb, when not a word in it refers to Jesus? The answer to this question may be found in the Jewish expectation that the call for a new song, which comes from the Psalms (see comments on 5:9), cannot be answered until the days of the Messiah have come. Singing a new song, therefore, has its roots in the belief that Jesus is the Messiah. In this way the song of Moses is also the song of the Lamb.

The song of Moses (Exod. 15) is sung *after* the righteous judgments of God have been made known. The ten plagues in Egypt culminated in the downfall of Pharaoh and his army. The song of Moses and the Lamb is sung *before* the seven bowls filled with plagues were poured out over the earth and the Roman empire collapsed. Revelation is so sure of God's victory that it can be celebrated in song, in advance, by anticipation. The sign in heaven is great and marvelous (15:1). That is true also of God's deeds (15:3).

SEVEN BOWLS 15:5–16:21

Just as after the singing that followed the sounding of the seventh trumpet heaven opened and the ark of the covenant became visible as the throne of the holy God (11:19), so now after the song of the victors heaven opens and the seven angels holding the seven bowls full of the wrath of God appear. These bowls are poured out one after another. There is some haste to get to the end. There are only two short interruptions: the voice from the altar (16:7) and the warning to be watchful (16:15). The catastrophes are almost identical with those in Revelation 8 and 9, and the order in which they occur is the same. The images of misfortune are repeated; almost all of them have been used before. It is hard to devise many new comparisons. That is not to say, however, that they do not exist. Our own time could provide new illustrations.

15:5-8 SMOKE IN THE TEMPLE

Following the song of Moses and the Lamb the door to the heavenly sanctuary—here [not in RSV, but see NIV and KJV] called by its Old Testament name "the tabernacle of the testimony" (Exod. 38:21)—is opened. The seven angels, dressed in priestly clothing (2 Chron. 5:12) and, like Christ (1:13), wearing golden sashes around their chests, come out of the temple. One of the four living creatures (4:6ff.) hands the seven golden bowls full of the anger of God to the seven angels. This is the crucial moment, the beginning of the end. The temple is filled with smoke (Isa. 6:4) and no one can enter into it (Exod. 40:34-35). The sanctuary, which had opened (11:19; 15:5), is now closed. The judgments of God can no longer be averted—neither by prayers nor by appeals for his mercy. God is not available for conversation with anyone anymore; not until Rome and its emperor have disappeared from the earth for good.

16:1-11 FIVE BOWLS

At God's command seven angels come forward to pour out bowls filled with the anger of God (Jer. 10:25; Zeph. 3:8). First the earth is affected. The worshipers of the emperor are troubled with malignant sores. Next, the sea is affected: all marine life dies. Then the water in springs and rivers is made undrinkable.

These disasters have their prototypes in the plagues of Egypt (Exod. 9:10-11; 7:17-21). The angel in charge of the drinking water repeats a passage from the song of Moses and of the Lamb concerning the righteousness and holiness of God (15:3-4). An eye for an eye: the worshipers of the Beast and his image have shed blood; now they will have to drink their own blood (Isa. 49:26). They will kill each other (6:4). The heavenly altar agrees with the angel and confirms the justice of the judgment of God. In a vision even an altar can speak.

With the outpouring of the fourth bowl, God permits the sun to scorch the people. After all, the sun is not a god, as the nations think, but a humble servant of God; it does what God tells it to do. People blaspheme God. The sores cause fever, and there is no drinking water. And then this awful heat comes on top of it all. And if this were not enough, God reaches out to the throne of the Beast. The divine emperor cannot stop his kingdom from becoming pitch dark (Exod. 10:21-23). This darkness really hurts. How is that possible? If we assume that the Egyptian darkness was caused by a sandstorm coming out of the wilderness and lasting three days there is a ready explanation. People are forced to swallow sand. They are biting their dehydrated tongues. This leads to oral infections on top of the sores they already had. But even this does not produce conversion. In the sun's heat, butter melts but clay hardens.

16:12-16 THE SIXTH BOWL

By drying out the great river Euphrates the sixth angel opens a road for the kings of the East. John here has the Old Testament in mind, where Cyrus, the Persian king, captured Babylon. The sword came over Babylon—its boasters, its heroes, its army, its treasures—and over its waters so that they dried out (Jer. 50:35-38). God raised up Cyrus as a conquering king from the East. He caused the rivers to dry up and called Cyrus his shepherd (Isa. 44:27-28). Just as Cyrus the Persian (Dan. 6:28) conquered Babylon, so the Parthians will bring about the downfall of Rome, the new Babylon.

But beside the Parthian threat to Rome on the eastern

boundary of the empire, John sees something else. The frog plague (Exod. 8:1-15) triggers this vision. Instead of an army of frogs, though, only three appear: one out of the mouth of the Dragon, another out of the mouth of the Beast, and still another out of the mouth of the beast, the false prophet. It is this Roman triumvirate that produces the evil spirits—unclean powers that, because they are linked with the devil, are able, by their miracles, to lead people astray (13:13-14). These evil spirits come in the form of frogs. In the ancient Persian religion, Ahriman was the god of evil who created the frog, among other creatures, and sometimes assumed the form of a frog. These evil spirits will proceed to mobilize the nations of the entire earth. On the great Day, the world will be unified in waging war against the Christians (20:8-9).

The kings and their peoples come together at a place that in Hebrew is called Harmageddon or Armageddon. Specific details are lacking here, however. Where is it? What does the name mean? The other Hebrew word we encountered, "Abaddon" (9:11), was translated into Greek, presumably by a copyist. The fact that this was not done here may be an indication that the copyists were nonplussed by the expression. There are three possibilities:

1. *Har Mageddon*, or (the) Mount Megiddo. The city of Megiddo was situated at the southwestern edge of a great plain, the Plain of Megiddo. Present-day Megiddo is a hill of ruins called Tell el-Mutesellim (hill of the governor). Israel was not able to capture Megiddo, along with many other cities, from the Canaanites (Judg. 1:27). This venture only succeeded under David. Solomon appointed twelve district governors (1 Kings 4:7). Governor Baana, son of Ahilud, administered Taanach and Megiddo, Bethshean and the country below Jezreel (1 Kings 4:12). Megiddo was one of the "chariot cities" that Solomon built (1 Kings 9:15-19; 10:26-29; 2 Chron. 9:25). The remains of horse stables were excavated in 1928. The possibility that Revelation should have intended the reading "Har Mageddon" is excluded. Megiddo is not a mountain, nor is it situated on a mountain.

2. *Ar Mageddon*, or (the) city Megiddo. The Hebrew *Ar* in this case begins with an *ayin*. Megiddo was an important city, which is frequently mentioned in the Old Testament. The kings of Canaan fought by the waters of Megiddo (Judg. 5:19); Ahaziah at one time fled in the direction of Megiddo

(2 Kings 9:27); Josiah died in battle at Megiddo (2 Kings 23:29; 2 Chron. 35:20-27). Every year laments were raised to commemorate the death of this devout king (2 Chron. 35:25). In Jerusalem the mourning over someone who was pierced would be as great as that over Hadad-rimmon in the Plain of Megiddo (Zech. 12:11). From extra-biblical sources we know that Megiddo, which was located strategically on the main road between Egypt and Mesopotamia, was a powerfully fortified city. But since 350 B.C. the place was a heap of ruins. It is hard to imagine that this place, which slid into oblivion, would be the rallying point for the armies of the anti-God powers.

Moreover, Megiddo nowhere occurs in eschatological contexts. The final war takes place either on the mountains of Israel (Ezek. 38:21; 39:2-4) or in the valley of Jehoshaphat (Joel 3:2, 12), also called the valley of decision (Joel 3:14). Satan's ultimate attempt to eradicate the church of Christ is linked with the prophecies of Ezekiel 38 and 39. This the names of Gog and Magog prove. But in Revelation there is no reference to the mountains of Israel as the final battlefield of history. (For the valley of Jehosphaphat, the valley of decision, see comments on 14:20.)

3. *Ar Mageddon.* The Hebrew *Ar* in this case begins with an *aleph*. It is generally assumed that the mysterious place where the nations will meet has something to do with Hadad-rimmon in the Plain of Megiddo (Zech. 12:11). But that is usually as far as it goes. Still, here one may find the key to the solution of the problem, which needs to be sought with the aid of something called *gematria.* * Here we mean that when two different words add up to the same numerical value, they can be equated. Earlier we considered the numerical value of a word in connection with the number of the beast (cf. 13:18). The numerical value of the Hebrew name "Hadad-rimmon" (Zech. 12:11) totals 309. The numerical value of the Hebrew word for "the decision" is also 309. Omitting the article, one gets a total of 304, which is precisely the numerical value of Ar Mageddon (beginning with the *aleph*). And therefore we get this sequence: "Ar Mageddon" equals "the valley

---

*The author here uses the word *isipsephie,* for which there is, to my knowledge, no English equivalent. My translation "gematria" is inferred from the context.—*Trans.*

of decision" which is "the valley of Jehoshaphat" (Joel 3:2, 12, 14).

To that valley the Lord God will gather the nations, and there he will judge them (Joel 3:2). It is God who summons the nations to a holy war (Joel 3:9). The Day of the Lord is near (Joel 3:14), the great and dreadful Day of the Lord (Joel 2:31). These concepts occur also in Revelation 16:14: "to assemble" [RSV] or "to gather" [NIV], "war," "the great day." We may add that the term "the great day" from Joel 2:31 (apart from the quotation in Acts 2:20) occurs in the New Testament only here in 16:14. The importance to John of Joel's prophecy is demonstrated in 14:14-20.

On the basis of these considerations I believe that we must read 16:16 as Ar Mageddon, not as Har Mageddon. The three unclean spirits assembled the nations. The Plain of Megiddo would be a good rallying point. John calls the place of meeting Ar Mageddon, using a code word. This is a practice still followed by general staffs of armies. The church, too, has resorted to the use of code language. In the days of the Reformation, Antwerp was called "the vineyard," Brussels "the sun," Ghent "the sword" and Doornik "the palm tree." From a human point of view the demons blow the trumpet to gather the nations. But to Revelation it is God who drives the kings of the entire world, together with their armies, into the valley with the symbolic name, the valley of Jehoshaphat, the valley of decision, for the purpose of settling accounts. Grammatically one could translate the words of 16:16 like this: "they (the spirits) assembled. . . ." But the translation "He (the Lord God) assembled . . ." seems to me to deserve preference. That is how Joel reads: "I will gather all the nations" (3:2).

In chapter 16, verse 15 seems to disturb the coherence of the material. For that reason the suggestion has been made to insert it between the third and the fourth verse of chapter 3, where it would fit very well. Nevertheless, it also fits very well the announcement of the great Day of the Lord (16:14). The return of Christ belongs to that day, and a warning to the churches is not out of place here. The person who goes to sleep "without taking off his clothes," as it were, is to be congratulated. Then when Jesus returns like a thief in the night he does not have to run into the street naked. In Israel, nakedness was regarded, all nudism notwithstanding, as something of which one should be ashamed (3:18). God provided clothing for Adam and Eve after they lost their Paradisal legacy.

16:17-21 THE SEVENTH BOWL

The contents of the last bowl are poured out upon the atmosphere. The effect of this bowl remains hidden. But God does observe that the mandate given to the seven angels (16:1) has been fulfilled. It is now time to execute judgment over Babylon.

The phenomena of thunder and lightning, gusts of wind, and earthquakes (4:5; 8:5; 11:19) belong to the appearances of God [theophanies]. The earthquake that occurs is unparalleled in history (Dan. 12:1). The great city, which is usually Babylon, is Jerusalem here (see the comments on 11:8). The capital of Israel breaks apart in three sections and the capitals of the nations turn into ruins. Islands and mountains are moved (6:14). Enormous hailstones, dwarfing those which fell in Egypt (Exod. 9:24), come down out of the sky. But the people do not repent. They blaspheme God. Earlier, when Jerusalem was ravaged by an earthquake and 10 percent of the houses collapsed, people became afraid and acknowledged their sins (11:13). But here their hearts are hardened.

When Jerusalem is split in three parts and other capitals are destroyed, someone reminds God of the fact that he planned to give to Babylon, that other great city, the cup brimming with the heady wine of his wrath (14:10). Who is it that reminds God of this threat? It is left unsaid. [RSV and NIV render this "God remembered."] It could be the court of heaven (Dan. 7:10). In 18:5 it is not others who remind God of Babylon's iniquity but God himself who remembers it. To pretend that God had forgotten to punish Babylon is a way of telling a story. It is characteristically human to reason that it would be unjust to condemn Jerusalem and other cities while sparing Rome. But Rome is definitely not going to go scot-free. It is now Rome's turn.

THE DESTRUCTION OF THE GREAT CITY
17:1–19:10

The seven bowls are empty. Babylon will now fall. First, John depicts the great city as a prostitute seated on a scarlet beast (chap. 17). Next, he describes in detail the fall of Rome (chap. 18). After that a song of praise celebrating the downfall of Babylon is raised and the wedding of the Lamb is announced (19:1-10).

17:1-6a THE WOMAN ON THE BEAST

One of the angels having the seven bowls invites John to come up to show him the coming judgment over the city of Rome. This city is described as an important prostitute—a metaphor that was used for other cities as well: Nineveh (Nah. 3:4), Tyre (Isa. 23:15-18), and even Jerusalem (Ezek. 16:35). Kings commit adultery with these public women (Isa. 23:17) and people were intoxicated with their lewd wine (Jer. 51:7; Rev. 14:8). To say that this prostitute is seated by many waters is a bit overdone when applied to the city of Rome by the Tiber, although it does describe Babylon (Jer. 51:13) and is projected back on Rome.

In the Spirit, John is carried by an angel into the wilderness. The woman he sees there is seated on a scarlet beast that has seven heads and ten horns and is full of blasphemous names. This expresses her kinship with the blood-red Dragon that has seven heads and ten horns (12:3), and with the Beast that has ten horns and seven heads bearing blasphemous names (13:1). While this is not an identification with them, the imitation is unmistakable. The woman is arrayed in purple and scarlet. Purple is the color of royalty, and scarlet is the color of the beast on which she rides. By these touches the demonic character of this kingship is indicated. She wears golden jewels, precious stones, and pearls: wealth reminiscent of that of the other prostitute, the city of Tyre (Ezek. 28:13).

One may question why John sees this woman in a wilderness. The answer is that this anticipates the judgment to come. Babylon was destined to be a wilderness (Jer. 51:26). This is also the destiny of Rome because, in her hand, she holds a golden cup full of perversities and lewd impurities. Leviticus 18 lists a series of dishonorable actions that are an abomination to the Lord God. Prostitution is frequently a metaphor for idolatry. But this link by no means excludes a variety of sexual sins.

The woman has on her forehead an unflattering name. Just as the devil is the father of lies (John 8:44)—that is, the arch-liar—so Rome is the mother of prostitutes, a phrase one can render as "arch-prostitute." The reader of the book and the listening church (1:3) are reminded that "Babylon the great" must not be taken literally, but is code-language. This has gradually become almost unnecessary, however. The woman who has drunk the blood of the saints and of the witnesses to Jesus as though it were wine can be no other than Rome. Earth-dwellers became drunk with the wine of her fornication (17:2); the woman is drunk with the blood of Christians. It is really not a mystery that the woman on the beast is Rome. The real mystery is the animal on which she rides (17:8ff.)!

17:6b-14 THE SECRET

The same angel who invited John to come up (17:1) now asks him why he is so astonished. He does not wait for an answer, however, but immediately begins to explain the beast with the seven heads and the ten horns.

The angel says that the beast was, now is not, and will come (1:4, 8; 4:8). God is the God of the past, the present, and the future, and in that regard is unique. People come and go. Our lifespan is seventy or eighty years (Ps. 90:10), and occasionally one makes it to a hundred. The only one who has existed for centuries is Satan. And of him the beast is a smaller model.

In this case the beast is Nero. He "was" emperor. He committed suicide, however, and so "he is not." People did not believe he was dead but thought he would return; thus, he "is coming." And all those whose names have not been recorded from the beginning of the creation in the book of life (13:8) will marvel when Nero returns. It had been reported earlier that the whole world was astonished that the Roman empire recovered from the deadly wound caused by the suicide of the emperor (13:3). John now prophesies that Nero is coming and is going to meet his doom.

As far as the seven heads are concerned, this is a riddle that will prove who is intelligent (remember 13:18). The seven heads are seven mountains, on which the woman sits. To solve this riddle one does not have to be very clever. The reference is to Rome, the city built on seven hills.

But this is not all. The seven heads are also seven emperors. Five are dead. The fifth was Nero. That is the given from which we must proceed. From that point we must calculate backward and forward. The list then looks like this:

1. Augustus		27 B.C.—A.D.	14
2. Tiberius	A.D. 14	—	37
3. Caligula	37	—	41
4. Claudius	41	—	54
5. Nero	54	—	68

Then follows a period under Galba, Otho, and Vitellius, which is skipped as being unimportant.

6. Vespasian	69	—	79
7. Titus	79	—	81
8. Domitian	81	—	96

There "were" five. Number six now "is." The seventh is coming. From this the conclusion has sometimes been drawn that Revelation must be situated and dated in the reign of emperor Vespasian. But the fact that John knows that the reign of emperor Titus has been of only short duration (A.D. 79-81) and that he fixes the reader's attention on the eighth emperor is an argument that supports a date for Revelation in the reign of Domitian. This number eight belongs to the seven predecessors and is the Nero who has come back from the dead, the beast that "was" and "is not" and "is coming" (17:8). And just as the twenty-four elders thank God Almighty "who is and who was," and say nothing of his "coming" because God has already come, so also the beast is described: "he was and now is not." The "coming" or the "will be" is no longer necessary (17:11), because Nero has reappeared in the person of Domitian. Little good is to be expected from the eighth king. But here, too, John repeats what he prophesied in 17:8: the beast is going to his destruction.

The ten horns are ten kings. They are not really kings but for the duration of one hour they receive royal power to help the beast. Unitedly they put their power and might at the disposal of the beast for the war against the Lamb. The soldiers of Christ are those who have been called and chosen by him and will be his faithful followers.

The war is won in so short a time—in one hour the issue is settled—because the Lamb is Lord of lords and King of kings—Hebrew superlatives for the supreme Lord and greatest King. This is one of the titles of God (Deut. 10:17; Dan. 2:47; 1 Tim. 6:15) also conferred on Christ (Rev. 17:14; 19:16). Revelation uses it as a method to indicate Christ's equality with God.

We cannot determine with absolute certainty what John had in mind with the ten kings who were not kings. Scholars have suggested they were satraps, the heads of the provinces of the kingdom of the Parthians. The idea was that Nero would wreak vengeance on Rome with the aid of Persian armies. But because their specific object is to persecute Christians, they must have been the governors of the provinces of the Roman empire, who had rallied behind the banners of the beast. This suspicion is supported by the sequel where still another interpretation of the woman on the beast is offered.

17:15-18 ANOTHER INTERPRETATION

The governors and the Beast have lost the war against the Lamb. And then, as happens quite often after a defeat, rebellion breaks out. First the ten kings placed themselves unitedly, and with all their power, behind the emperor (the Beast) (17:13). Now, however, they again unitedly transfer their royal powers to a man (the beast) who will thrust Domitian from the throne in order to become emperor himself. The beast (the new man) and the ten horns (the governors of the Roman provinces) will hate the prostitute by the waters. That woman is the great city of Rome, and the waters are the many nations inside the empire. They will take from the prostitute all her jewels, the purple, and scarlet (17:4), so that she will be destitute and naked. They will eat parts of her flesh (cf. Micah 3:2, 3) and burn the rest. This pictures in metaphorical language the plundering of Rome. Thus revolution devours its own children.

According to John this rebellion was not conceived by man but by God. This is not something either the pretender to the crown or the governors themselves know. But in this vision it is God himself who put it in their hearts. They will perform the purpose of God until all his words have been realized. God firmly holds the reins of world rule in his hand. Not the emperor, not the revolutionary, not the governors, not the heads of the scarlet beast, not the ten horns—but God rules.

As to the downfall of Rome, there are differences within the book. There is, on the one hand, the expectation that the Parthians will destroy the empire (6:2; 16:12); on the other, there is the expectation that rebellion from within will put an end to it (17:15-18). This evidences a certain ambivalence. But for John it is clear that God and the Lamb will carry out judgment over Rome, the city that persecutes the Christians. What will happen to Rome is what happened to the fourth beast in the Book of Daniel: the court will sit, and Rome's power will be taken away and completely destroyed (Dan. 7:26).

In the Conclusion we shall reflect on the fact that the history of the first centuries after Christ, meanwhile, turned out differently from the way John prophesied.

18:1-8 THE FALL OF BABYLON

Chapter 18 simply proceeds from the assumption that Rome's verdict has been passed. A special angel with enormous authority, at whose descent the dark earth becomes light, proclaims with a powerful voice so that all can hear: Babylon has fallen (cf. comments on 14:8). It has become a ruin where demons, evil spirits, and unclean birds dwell. That prospect had been foretold by the prophets (Isa. 13:21-22; 34:13-15; Jer. 50:39; a list of unclean birds occurs in Deut. 14:12-19). The cause of Babylon's downfall, referred to already in 14:8 and 17:2, is repeated (18:3).

Because Babylon's downfall is certain, the people of God are urgently advised to leave the city before it is too late (Jer. 51:6, 9, 45). Otherwise, these people may suffer along with the rest for the city's sins; for anyone who stays will perish (Gen. 19:15). In Jeremiah the people of God in Babylon were the exiles residing there (Jer. 51:45). For John the people of God are believers in Christ. Since Babylon is Rome and the people of God are the church of Jesus Christ, the advice is directed to Christians—flee from Rome!

Rome cannot be saved anymore. Its sins have piled up as high as heaven (Jer. 51:9; cf. Ezra 9:6). God has remembered her crimes. The church is warned to leave Rome as quickly as possible; the city's enemies are exhorted to pay her back what she has given (Jer. 50:29; Ps. 137:8). Even more strongly, they are to pay her back double for what she has done (Jer. 16:18). Pride goes before a fall. This proud queen, who thought she would never become a mourning wife or mother or a widow, will lose her husband and family in one day as a result of plagues that strike her (Isa. 47:8-9). The emperor and the inhabitants of Rome will die and the city itself will be burned (17:16; 18:9, 18). The fact that God is mighty is the guarantee that the judgment will be carried out (Jer. 50:34).

18:9-19 LAMENTATION BY KINGS, MERCHANTS, AND SEAFARING PEOPLE

The mourners can begin to sing their dirges: God has firmly decided to bring about Rome's downfall. John mentions three categories of people here—kings, merchants, and seafaring folk—which he borrowed, along with their songs of lament, from Ezekiel 27, where a funeral song is sung over Tyre. In Revelation the lament contains three elements: (1) people keep their distance from the burning city from fear of suffering the same fate; (2) they remember the riches of the past; and (3) they cry "How terrible! How terrible!" with regard to the city that became a heap of ruins in one hour's time.

Kings think of their political power. Merchants recall all the variety of their merchandise. Captains and sailors throw dust on their heads and ask who can be compared with the city. It is the same question that the earthdwellers raised with respect to the Beast: "Who can match it?" (13:4). The reference to the Beast is not meant in terms of harbors and fleets as much as military superiority.

18:20-24 THE PUNISHMENT

Following the threefold "woe!" comes the simple and single song of joy from heaven (the angels), the saints (Dan. 7:22, 25, 27), the apostles (Peter and Paul had died a martyr's death under Nero), and the prophets (protesting emperor worship). They had won a victory in the contest with Babylon. And Babylon will get her just reward. Symbolically, the downfall of Babylon is represented by a millstone that is cast into the sea, never to come up again. Jeremiah once performed a similar ritual (Jer. 51:63-64).

Judgment will be complete. Just notice the fivefold "never . . . again." Never again will merriment and song be heard

(Isa. 24:8; Ezek. 26:13). Never again will the skilled trades be practiced. Never again will the sound of grinding be heard. Never again will lamps shine in the house. Never again will there be a wedding (Jer. 25:10). And that for three reasons:

1. The life of Babylon was one of luxury, because highly placed people went shopping there. But wealth is dangerous—it often goes to people's heads.
2. Babylon wove a magic spell with her love potions. With the heady wine of her adulteries (14:8; 17:2, 4) she seduced people to take part in emperor worship.
3. To Babylon's conscience clung the blood of the saints (6:10; 16:6; 17:6; 19:2) who had been slain like animals there (Jer. 51:49).

19:1-10 HALLELUJAH!

In anticipation of the fall of Babylon songs of lament had been raised; now, in anticipation of God's action as though he had already avenged the blood of his servants, a song of praise is lifted up and, proleptically, as though it had already arrived, the glory to come is celebrated.

The Hebrew word *Hallelujah* is striking here; this is the only instance of it in the entire New Testament. It gives a special emphasis to the songs of praise. The great Day is now very close. That which could be read on the final pages of the sealed scroll (5:1-7) is now being carried out. The twenty-four elders and the four living creatures, who were eyewitnesses of the transfer of the scroll to the Lamb (5:8-14), say "amen" to the song and repeat the Hallelujah.

The songs reach back also to the things uttered in the preceding chapters. The cry of the souls under the altar "to avenge their blood" (6:10) has now been answered—almost. That God's judgments are true and just is something the altar has already said (16:7). The smoke over the burning city of Babylon is one of the many themes of the song of lament sung by the kings and seafaring people (18:8, 18). Earlier (14:11), an angel announced that the pall of smoke hanging in the sky was going to remain forever.

Now John introduces a new element: the wedding feast of the Lamb. Its source lies in the Song of Solomon, which the Jews understood as symbolic of the covenant that God, the bridegroom, had with his people Israel, the bride. Christians applied the meaning to Christ and his church. And since in Jewish law the bride was legally considered a spouse, one could mention the wife of the Bridegroom.

In contrast to the arch-whore Babylon, with her wealth and finery (17:4), the Bride wears a garment of fine linen, bright and clear: a combination of simplicity and purity. Just as John explained the bowl full of incense ("there are the prayers of the saints"; 5:8), he adds a note of explanation here: the Bride's ornament is her obedience to the commandments of God. Deeds are "righteous" when done in agreement with the covenant and the law. The people of the saints of the Most High (Dan. 7:22, 25, 27) was faithful Israel embodied in Daniel and his friends and now present in the Bride, the wife of the Lamb. The angel commands John to write down congratulations. On an earlier occasion the dead who died in the Lord were also congratulated (14:13). This time the guests who are invited to the wedding feast of the Lamb are called happy.

The angel, who has shown to John the coming judgment over the great prostitute (17:1), now solemnly assures him that all these words (from 17:1 to 19:9) are the true words of God. So far in Revelation this had not yet been affirmed and advanced with such emphasis. Words from God himself! John wants to throw himself at the feet of the angel to worship him, but the angel forbids him. Like John, and like the prophets and the brothers, an angel is a servant of God. Worship is due, but not to the servant, only to God. There is a parallel statement at the close of the book (22:6-9).

The "brothers" are characterized as those who hold to the testimony of Jesus. This is a reference back to the beginning of the revelation. Through an angel Jesus has shown John the things that will soon take place. This is what makes the Book of Revelation a prophecy (1:1-3). That which the Spirit has to say is identical with the testimony of Jesus. And this is the criterion by which to discriminate between true and false prophecy. That which the beast prophesied, and confirmed with signs, and was so enormously successful with (13:11-18), was the work of a false prophet (16:13; 19:20; 20:10). Through John the brothers have received the testimony of Jesus. Let them hold fast to it.

THE FINAL WAR 19:11–20:10

Christ, the Rider on the white horse, followed by his own militia, also riding white horses, now advances to defeat the armies of the enemy (19:11-16). The Beast and the false prophet are taken prisoner and thrown alive into hell. Their armed forces are slaughtered and remain behind on the battlefield for the vultures (19:7-21). The Dragon is seized and chained for a thousand years (20:1-3). Martyrs come to live and rule with Christ for a thousand years (20:4-6). After that Satan is set loose and then, following a final futile effort on his part to crush the church, thrown into hell. The armies of Gog and Magog are destroyed by fire from heaven (20:7-10).

19:11-16 THE RIDER ON THE WHITE HORSE

Finally, after so many visions and anticipations, the decisive battle will be fought. John sees heaven open and Christ coming out as a Rider on horseback. Although his horse is white, the resemblance to the rider on the white horse in 6:2 is only superficial. The heavenly Rider bears the name Faithful and True. He is the faithful and true Witness (3:14) whose judgment is just (Isa. 11:3-4), something he has in common with God (Pss. 96:13; 98:9; Rev. 16:7; 19:2). And because he is a righteous Judge he wages war against anti-Christian forces. His eyes are ablaze. Nothing escapes his awesome scrutiny. The eyes are holy—as in the vision of the call (1:14).

On his crowns is inscribed a name that, though it can be read, cannot be understood. Only the person who bears it knows what it means (2:17). This, however, does not apply to the other names: "the Word of God" (John 1:1), "the greatest King," and "the highest Lord" (17:14). The most accurate personal name, which expresses his true being, has not yet been made known. God has not yet revealed everything. But what he has said and done is more than enough for people to endure in the world.

Coming from heaven with Christ are the armies that follow him on white horses and in white clothes. Out of the mouth of Christ comes a sharp sword with which he slays the nations (1:16); he rules over them with a rod of iron (2:27; 12:5); he tramples out the wine in the winepress from which the heady wine of God's anger flows (14:19-20); his robe is spattered with blood (Isa. 63:1-6). So reads the graphic depiction of the triumphant Rider on the white horse in his bloody war against the Beast, the beast, and the kings and their armies. He does not bear his name in vain; the highest Lord and the greatest King is rightly written on his robe and on the leg of his boot.

19:17-21 THE DEFEAT OF THE BEAST AND
THE FALSE PROPHET

An angel, standing on the sun as his platform, invites all the birds (listed in Deut. 14:12-19) to a meal that God has prepared (Ezek. 39:4, 17-20). God is giving the birds a feast and a treat. They will glut themselves on the dead bodies of defeated soldiers (Matt. 24:28), the army of the Beast, the kings, and their warriors, who have assembled to wage war against the Rider on the white horse and his soldiers (16:14, 16). But the Lamb will overcome his enemies (17:14); they do not have a chance. The Beast (13:1-10) and the false prophet (13:11-18) are taken prisoner and thrown alive into the fire of hell. We are not told who it is who throws them into the volcanic lake of burning sulfur. Very likely it is not Christ himself; more likely it was his militia who did the job. It was not God but Michael and his angels who thrust the Dragon and his angels from heaven (12:7-9). It was not Christ but an angel who chained the Dragon (20:2). So it is here.

The two main characters, the Beast and the false prophet, go to hell alive. The others die by the sword of the Messiah (19:5). With the breath of his lips he kills the wicked (Isa. 11:4). Of the entire army not a soul escapes death.

20:1-3 THE DRAGON IS LOCKED UP

The Beast and the false prophet have been eliminated. But as long as the Dragon, the Serpent from Paradise, the devil, the Satan (cf. 12:9), has not been destroyed, the danger is not past and the victory is incomplete. He will again persuade the nations to make war against the Christians (20:3, 8). Therefore an angel descends from heaven with the key to the subterranean prison (9:1). He takes hold of the Dragon, chains him with a heavy chain, throws him into prison, locks it, and seals it over his head, so that he cannot get out. Finally the earth is at rest.

But this rest lasts only for a "thousand" years. This peace

is not definitive; it is a pause between two wars. After a thousand years Satan "has to" be released for a short while. Why does this "have to" be done? Would it not have been more simple to throw Satan into the lake of fire at once? Later this is what was done in any case (20:1). Why not immediately?

The answer is that this has to do with the plan of God, the blueprint of which we find in the Old Testament. Not only the kings of the earth will be locked up but also "the powers in the heavens above" (Isa. 24:21-23). Satan, according to Jewish interpretation, belongs to that heavenly army. This incarceration serves as pretrial detention until the day of judgment (2 Pet. 2:4; Jude 6). But in Revelation Satan regains his freedom for a short while.

This release is necessary, since it follows from the prophecies of Ezekiel (chaps. 38 and 39). Gog, the chief prince of Magog, will, together with many nations, storm into the land of Palestine and attack the people of Israel. That is a part of the final period of history. There is still another extreme attempt to eliminate the people of God. Satan will fire up Gog and Magog and their allies against the church.

20:4-6 THE MILLENNIUM

After the vision of the imprisonment of Satan, John sees thrones. Plural! These thrones are to be distinguished from the great white throne of God (20:11). Who are the ones sitting on these thrones? We are not told. But this we must fill in from our understanding of a parallel situation described in Daniel 7, where God sits down on his throne and the court sits on their thrones (7:9-10). Therefore, it is a court session. The dead will be raised to appear before God and to hear the verdict of the court (20:11-15). We should observe that only the dead are judged, and that by God. Judgment of the living has already taken place. The armies who followed the Beast have been killed by the sword of the Rider on the white horse (19:21). Gog and Magog, together with their nations, have been consumed by fire from heaven (20:9). The others' turn is still coming (21:8, 27). The Son of Man has put his sickle into the earth and harvested it (14:14-15). In the letters to the seven churches (chaps. 2 and 3), the return of Christ relates to the church and its members. This is also the case in 16:15, where not a word is said about the dead. The only exception, perhaps, is 1:7, which mentions those who have pierced him. In the Epilogue the final judgment is bound up with the return, but, again, this applies only to the living (22:12-15).

After the court has been seated, something remarkable happens. John sees the souls of the martyrs (for the word *souls* see discussion on 6:9-11) who were beheaded for the testimony of Jesus and the Word of God (1:2; 19:10). They refused to worship the Beast and his image, and to receive his mark (13:16; 14:9, 11; 16:2; 19:20). Some commentators think that the reference here is to two groups, martyrs and deceased Christians. In my opinion, only one category of people is intended. The martyrs are given special status because they have paid for their faith with their lives. Christians who have died a natural death rise at the same time as the other dead and are then judged (20:11-15). If all believers took part in what John calls the first resurrection, then there would be no need at the last judgment to open any books or to consult the book of life. Then God would need only to damn those who were left.

John sees how the martyrs come alive. The dead bodies begin to stir. They rise in order to exercise royal rule with Christ. That which applies to all believers, namely, that they are a kingdom of priests (1:6; 5:10), is granted to the martyrs a thousand years earlier, as compensation for the suffering they have endured for Christ's sake. That is, as compensation for their imprisonment and torture, they arise before the rest. This is called the first resurrection to distinguish it from the general resurrection of the dead.

Therefore the martyrs are not only called "happy"; they are also declared "holy." "Holy" is the name Isaiah gives to those who are left in Zion and are recorded among the living in Jerusalem (Isa. 4:3). They are secured against the power of the second death (2:11; 20:14; 21:8). The first death is the human process of dying; the second is hellfire (20:14; 21:8).

In the Conclusion we shall return to the doctrine of the millennium.

20:7-10 THE DRAGON SET LOOSE

After a thousand years Satan is set free. He swiftly goes out to the nations at the borders of the world. He succeeds in persuading Gog and Magog (Ezek. 38 and 39) to be the leaders of the nations in "the four corners of the earth" (for this term, see the Introduction). In Ezekiel it is God himself who commands Gog, the chief prince of Magog, to attack Israel; in Revelation it is Satan who mobilizes the nations for a final assault on the church.

From the entire length and breadth of the earth they march up to Jerusalem, which is situated on an elevation. For that reason they "march up" [cf. RSV], a familiar expression among pilgrims (Luke 18:31). But pilgrims come with peaceful intentions; these enemies go up to surround the city. That also happened at the siege of Jerusalem (Luke 19:43). John avoids the name Jerusalem here, but "the beloved city" [KJV, RSV] is clearly Jerusalem (Pss. 78:68; 87:2; Jer. 11:15; 12:7). And just as the word "camp" (Exod. 29:14; Lev. 4:12, 21; 10:4-5; Heb. 13:11, etc.) is transferred to the church of Jesus Christ, so also is the honorable title "the beloved city."

The Christians are saved by a "fire from heaven" (Ezek. 38:22; 39:6) that consumes the attackers. The devil, who leads the nations astray (not "deceived," as in most versions, for when John writes the deception is still going on), is thrown into hell in order to suffer eternal punishment together with the Beast and the false prophet.

Looking back one can see that John, in chapter 20, is following the pattern established by the prophet Ezekiel.

1. First, by "resurrection of the dead" Ezekiel means the national revival of Israel (Ezek. 37:1-14). It is a metaphor for the beginning of a new existence as a nation. Skeletons from the valley of dry bones are fitted back together as bodies and begin to live again. John uses the very same verb, "they came to life" (Ezek. 37:10; Rev. 20:4), but he understands this "resurrection" literally as a resurrection from the dead. The martyrs arise from the dead.

2. Next Ezekiel prophesies that the northern kingdom (Israel) and the southern kingdom (Judah) will become one again and that God will return the Jews, who are now scattered over the entire world (the diaspora), to the land of Palestine as their home (Ezek. 37:15-28). Then "my servant David shall be king over them; . . . David my servant shall be their prince for ever" (37:24-25). That, then, is the messianic kingdom, which in John is the millennium.

3. After that, Israel, now united and living in peace, will be trampled underfoot in a surprise attack by the nations, led

by Gog from the land of Magog, the chief prince of Meshech and Tubal. But Gog and his armed gangs will be destroyed by a rain of burning sulfur (Ezek. 38:22). This is also what happens in Revelation to the assault on the camp of the saints and the beloved city. Gog and Magog are now combined in one ominous-sounding name that adds an extra dimension of terror to the apocalyptic menace.

THE FINAL JUDGMENT 20:11-15

When Satan has had all power taken from him for good, it is time for the resurrection from the dead and the final judgment. At the sight of God, the great Judge, heaven and earth flee away—reminiscent of Psalm 114:3, 7. The old heaven and the old earth will be destroyed (Ps. 102:26-27; Isa. 51:6; Matt. 24:35; Mark 13:31; Luke 21:33) to make room for the new heaven and the new earth (21:1). The renewal of the world is not a restoration of the present world but a new creation. Not a trace of the old world will be left (Dan. 2:35).

John sees the dead stand before the throne of God. The sea, death, and the abode of the dead give up the dead they hold. They are all judged according to what they have done. Heaven has kept precise records of the good and evil everyone has done. Books are opened (Dan. 7:10) and alongside of them is the book of life (3:5). Those whose names are not recorded there are lost.

The juxtaposition of the books in which human deeds are recorded and the book in which the names of believers are inscribed provides a visionary picture of the tension between personal responsibility and election. John comforts Christians who are being persecuted: Jesus has inscribed their names in the registers of the New Jerusalem. And John admonishes the church to remain faithful: to toy with grace is to forfeit it.

When death has been overcome and the abode of the dead no longer exists (Isa. 25:8; 1 Cor. 15:26, 54-55), a new beginning can be made.

THE HOLY CITY 21:1–22:5

In Revelation 20 John followed, for the most part, Ezekiel's outline: the resurrection of the dead (Ezek. 37), the messianic kingdom (Ezek. 37), and Gog and Magog (Ezek. 38 and 39). Ordinarily one would now expect the description of the new temple (Ezek. 40–48). Instead, after inserting the piece on the last judgment (20:11-15), John devotes all his attention to the New Jerusalem. Ezekiel deals summarily with that subject in a few verses (48:30-35). And the new temple, the description of which fills eight chapters in Ezekiel, is dismissed by John in just one line: "I did not see a temple in the city" (21:22)!

21:1-8 THE NEW JERUSALEM

The road for the salvation that was promised has now been paved. Heaven and earth have already fled (20:11), and not a trace of them could any longer be seen. They must make room for the new heaven and the new earth. We have no trouble seeing the necessity of a new earth. This old world, with its sin, death, and devil, cannot be harmonized with God's created design. But a new heaven? Indeed! The vault of heaven has also been damaged: its stars have fallen down like leaves from the trees (Isa. 34:4; Matt. 24:29; Mark 13:25; Luke 21:26; Rev. 6:13-14). And so there is talk of a new heaven. John here sees the new heaven and the new earth (Isa. 65:17; 66:22). The sea—that incubator and nursery of anti-God forces (13:1; Dan. 7:2-3)—is gone. That threat lies behind us.

Next, John gets to see the holy city (Isa. 52:1; Matt. 4:5), the New Jerusalem (3:12). He compares the city with a bride, adorned with her jewels (Isa. 61:10) and waiting for the bridegroom and his friends who are coming to get her. Elsewhere in Revelation the Bride was the church of Jesus Christ (19:7); here she is the New Jerusalem, destined to be God's domicile on earth. God dwells in heaven; now "heaven" comes down to earth. God is going to dwell among people. They will be his people, and he their God (Ezek. 37:27). Death will be no more (20:14); there will be no more tears (Isa. 25:8; Rev. 7:17); the sound of weeping and crying will be heard no more (Isa. 65:19), and there will be no more sorrow. All this must have warmed the hearts of the persecuted people. Their suffering is over. That belongs to the old order; it is something in the past tense.

God, seated on his throne, confirms this: "I am making everything new!" (NIV; cf. Isa. 43:19). John is told to write down that these words are trustworthy and true (19:9; 22:6).

God assures John that what he heard and saw (this refers to 21:1-4) has been realized. Again, this is a prophetic perfect (see the Introduction). Because it is established that God will do what he has said he will do, it may be assumed that salvation has already been realized. God is the Alpha and the Omega, the beginning and end (1:8), the God of the past, the present, and the future. To a person who is thirsty God will give water without cost (Isa. 55:1) from the springs of living— that is fresh, clear—water (Zech. 14:8). He will refresh these hunted souls (7:16-17). One who overcomes—the well-known formula from the letters to the seven churches (Rev. 2 and 3)— will inherit all this. And that which God had promised David ("I will be his father, and he shall be my son"; 2 Sam. 7:14; cf. Ps. 89:27-28) is now declared to be applicable to everyone who has not taken part in emperor worship.

But this is not true for the cowards who yielded to the temptation to give to the emperor that which is due only to God. Their fate is to be among unbelievers and lawbreakers (similar categories can be found in Deut. 18:9-14 and in Rom. 22:15); that is, in the second death, the fire of hell, the place of the Beast and the false prophet (19:20) and the devil (20:10). That is their inheritance, the counterpart of the inheritance received by those who overcame.

21:9-21 THE WALL, THE GATES, AND THE FOUNDATION

In chapter 16 John described the plagues that the seven angels with the seven bowls poured out upon the world. One of those angels had said to John, "Come, I will show you the punishment of the great prostitute" (NIV; 17:1). Now the same angel says: "Come, I will show you the Bride, the wife of the Lamb" (21:9). These two sentences form an antithetic parallel. The bride—legally the wife (19:7)—is placed over against the arch-prostitute (17:5).

There is still another resemblance—and contrast. In both cases the angel carries John away "in the Spirit": earlier, to the desert (17:3), to show him the great prostitute; then, to "a mountain great and high" to show him the Bride.

A third point of comparison concerns their respective ornaments. The prostitute has arrayed herself with golden ornaments, precious stones, and pearls (17:4), and the bride also has her ornaments. The difference, however, is that the first wears them to seduce the kings of the earth (17:2), while the second does so to please her husband (legally, the bridegroom is considered the spouse).

John has said already that he had seen the holy city, the New Jerusalem, come down from heaven (21:2). Now he returns to it. The angel had carried him to a large and high mountain, which becomes a lookout station from which he can survey a wide area. In this same way the devil had offered to Jesus a view of all the kingdoms known to the world (Matt. 4:8). Similarly, it was Moses' privilege, from Mount Nebo, to let his eyes range freely over the promised land (Deut. 3:27; 34:1). And Ezekiel sees a new temple from a high mountaintop (40:2).

From a similar lookout, then, John now describes the New Jerusalem. It is bathed in a sea of light because God, the source of light, is in its midst. For that reason it is a "city of light": it glitters like the most expensive gemstone.

Around the city is a wall with three gates to the East, three to the North, three to the South, and three to the West. On those gates the names of the twelve tribes of Israel were inscribed. In Ezekiel, too, the city wall has four times three gates and the gates bear the names of the twelve tribes of Israel (Ezek. 38:31-35). To John the New Jerusalem is the city where the Christians, the people of God, will live. In Revelation 7:4-8 the 144,000 who were sealed had been selected out of the twelve tribes of Israel as the core of the *militia Christi*. The twelve tribes stand for the church of Jesus Christ as a whole.

At each gate is an angel. It is not clear what those twelve angels are doing at the gates. Are they there only for ornamental reasons? That is not very likely. Must they sound the alarm at the approach of enemies? But all enemies are now gone and the gates will never again be closed (21:25). In Isaiah God has posted watchmen on the walls of Jerusalem, watchmen who will never be silent day or night (Isa. 62:6). It is their task to remind God continually of the glory [to come] of Jerusalem. But the New Jerusalem is already glorious from top to bottom. Is it their job to bar those who are not entitled to enter the city (21:27)? There is no way we can be certain.

The city wall was based on twelve enormous foundations on which the names of the twelve apostles were inscribed.

Was the name of Judas included? Or had the name of Matthias been substituted (Acts 1:26)? The text does not say. In Matthew the church is built on Peter the rock (Matt. 16:18); in Paul's writings it is built on Jesus Christ himself (1 Cor. 3:10), or has Christ as the cornerstone and the prophets and apostles as the foundation (Eph. 2:20); in Revelation the wall has been built on the twelve apostles of the Lamb. Each time the idea is the same: the foundation is the person and work of Jesus. And the name "Lamb" is richly suggestive of the atoning sacrifice offered on Golgotha.

John sees how the measurements of the city, its gates, and its wall, are taken. Earlier John himself had been told to plot the dimensions of the temple, the altar, and the temple square (11:1). One plots an area on which there is as yet no construction, but one measures that which has been built. In measuring the city the angel follows the example of the man with the measuring rod in the prophecies of Ezekiel, and takes measurements (Ezek. 42:15-20). The ground plan of the city is square, as in Ezekiel (48:16); the length, breadth, and height are exactly equal, each 12,000 stadia (for the distance see comments on 14:20). That is a megalopolis. The cube is the model of perfection. It rises high above the wall, which is 144 cubits high (a Jewish cubit is 46.2 cm.). The measures the angel uses are those currently in use among the people, but it could have been otherwise: just as God uses a different way of measuring time than we do (Ps. 90:4; 2 Pet. 3:8), so it could also be that God would use different space measurements.

The material of which the wall was made is jasper, and that of the city is gold so pure it is as if it were transparent glass; that is, it was not alloyed with anything else. The same is true of the pavement: it is the purest gold.

The city wall rests on twelve enormous foundations, each one consisting of one huge gemstone (cf. Isa. 54:11-12), each different from all the others. No two are alike. It is hard to determine what kind of precious stone John had in mind for every foundation. Therefore I have not translated the Greek names and have made no attempt to identify each stone. The main thing is the brilliance of the lowest part of the wall, and of the twelve gates, each of which consists of a giant pearl.

The ornaments of the woman on the scarlet beast (gold, precious stones, and pearls; 17:4) were used to show off her wealth. But in the New Jerusalem all this only serves the greater glory of the Lord God, the designer and builder of the heavenly city (Heb. 11:10).

21:22-27 A CITY WITHOUT A TEMPLE

In accordance with Jewish expectations, in the center of the holy city should have stood a temple surpassing by far those of Solomon and Herod in grandeur. But in John's vision there is no temple. We have discussed this before (11:1-13), but here it is underscored. Knowing the Jewish Christians' desire for a temple, the author of the Letter to the Hebrews has already worked out that theme: Jesus Christ is the High Priest who brought the perfect sacrifice for sin on Golgotha. And by that act the temple became superfluous. To John the Lord God and the Lamb are the temple. God no longer dwells in heaven but among the people (21:3). The temple is no longer necessary as a focus of revelation and a place of encounter. God does not just come down to his earthly residence now and then, but is uninterruptedly at work here below. The cloud is no longer the sign of his hidden and temporary presence (Exod. 40:34-38; Lev. 16:2; 1 Kings 8:10-11); the glory of God is now proof of his continuing and unconcealed presence.

For its light the New Jerusalem is no longer dependent on the sun and the moon, nor are lamps needed, either. This function is taken over by the Lamb—a fact from which no one ought to draw the conclusion that the Lamb (as lamp) is less than God (sun and moon). Christ's equality with God has been expressed repeatedly in Revelation. The predicates of the Father (the Alpha and the Omega, the first and the last, the beginning and the end; 1:8; 21:6) also belong to the Son (1:17; 2:8; 22:13). God's title of "the highest Lord and greatest King" is also ascribed to Jesus (17:14; 19:16).

In depicting the glory of the New Jerusalem, John freely uses the prophecy of Isaiah (Isa. 60:11-20). This, also, is the source of the idea that the sun and moon are redundant. The idea that the nations walk through its light is derived from the impression a person gets when looking at a city from a distance. In Isaiah the nations come to its light (Isa. 60:3) and come to the temple mountain to learn how to walk in the paths of God (Isa. 2:2-3). In Revelation they walk "through" [dia; RSV and NIV translate this "by"] its light.

It is difficult to follow the reasoning that the gates will

not be shut by day because there will be no night. In Isaiah the gates are always open and will never be closed—day or night (Isa. 60:11). But John's way of putting it is very compact: There will be no night there, so it is always day. And so the gates are never closed during those long days of twenty-four hours.

And because the gates are always open the stream of offerings that the kings of the earth are coming to bring can continue without interruption. This practice is to be understood not so much as the giving of presents as the transfer of taxes. Subjected kings were subject to tribute, which had to be paid yearly, both in money and in kind.

Until now not a good word had been spoken concerning the kings of the earth. They committed adultery with the Babylonian prostitute (17:2; 18:3, 9), who was mistress over them all (17:18). They made war on the saints (16:14) and against Christ (19:19). The nations, too, show up badly. They have drunk the heady wine of the Babylonian prostitute (14:8; 18:3) and have let themselves be deceived (18:23; 20:3, 8). But now witness the fulfillment of what had been celebrated in the song of Moses and the Lamb: "All nations will come and worship before you, for your righteous acts have been revealed" (NIV; 15:4). The Psalmist too had already sung of it (Ps. 86:9). Now that Babylon has fallen and the Beast, the false prophet, and the Dragon have been rendered harmless, only God and the Lamb are entitled to receive worship and service.

In the New Jerusalem nothing impure, no one who practices perversity or deception, will have access (cf. Rev. 22:15), for it is a holy city. The judgments of God have not led to the conversion of all people. But those who have hardened themselves are not admitted. Others may come and go like pilgrims. But only those whose names are inscribed in the Lamb's book of life (for the phrase, see comments on 13:8) may come and live in the New Jerusalem.

22:1-5 THE RIVER

In the remainder of his description of the New Jerusalem, John takes his cue from the river that in Ezekiel 47 springs up from under the threshold of the temple. In Revelation this river wells up out of the throne of God and the Lamb. We recall that there is no temple in the city (21:22). On each side of the river and right in the middle of the main street stand the trees of life. The one tree of life in Paradise, the one from which man was driven away (Gen. 2:9; 3:24), now returns in the form of many trees. Each month these trees bear fruit. The leaves have healing power in them, able to cure those who suffer from a variety of ailments and diseases. So the holy city is a medical center for the nations of the earth.

Nothing will ever again be struck by a curse (Zech. 14:11). Whatever was devoted to destruction is now devoted to God and so withdrawn from profane use. In the Old Testament, a curse entered the camp of Israel (Josh. 7:12) because Achan took something out of Jericho that was devoted to destruction. That curse was not lifted until Achan, with all he had, was stoned. But in the New Jerusalem all belongs to God and to the Lamb. All will serve him, look upon his face (Ps. 17:15), and bear his name.

To serve "him," to see "his" face, to bear "his" name: the reference is to God but not at the expense of the Lamb. It is the throne of God *and* of the Lamb (22:1, 3); God *and* the Lamb are the temple (21:22). To serve God is simultaneously to serve the Lamb. To see God is to see the Lamb. And on the foreheads of the 144,000 sealed ones there is written—notice the order—the name of the Lamb and the name of the Father (14:1).

Again we are told there will be no night there (22:5; cf. 21:25). It is a theme with variations:

1. There will be no night there; the moon is not necessary; is a lamp? No, the Lamb is the lamp; there is no need for the sun, for God shines with a bright light (21:23).
2. There will be no night there; so a day lasts twenty-four hours and therefore the gates do not have to be shut anymore (21:25).
3. There will be no night there; a day has twenty-four hours, so the light of lamps will not be necessary anymore. Will the sun always shine? No, for where God is, there the sun is not needed (22:5).

Then comes the fulfillment: the people of the saints of the Most High will receive the kingdom (Dan. 7:18, 22, 27). What was alluded to before (5:10; 20:6) will now become truth and reality.

EPILOGUE 22:6-21

As we mentioned in the Introduction, the epilogue refers back to the prologue (1:1-8). The central theme of the epilogue is the return of Christ.

The angel who has shown John the New Jerusalem (21:9) solemnly declares that everything that has been said about it (21:9–22:5) is completely true. God has sent his angel to reveal to his servants, the prophets, what must take place soon (1:1). John is one of those servants. God is Lord over the spirit of the prophets, hence also over John's spirit, and so John is a reliable prophet.

Christ himself confirms John's preaching by giving the assurance that his coming is very near (3:11). He underscores what John has written at the beginning of the book (1:3): Congratulations to those who obey the prophetic words of John.

John, as it were, himself underwrites it with his signature: I am he who has heard and seen the things written in the book. This man John was no stranger to the seven churches in Asia Minor. He was a man of authority. And that was the crucial point in the debate concerning the canonicity of the books of the Old and New Testaments. When people knew who the author was, or the authority behind the author, there were few problems. The churches knew John and there was no reason, therefore, to doubt his word. He was a man of God.

When John has heard the declaration of the angel, and especially the words of confirmation from Christ, he is impelled to throw himself at the feet of the angel who has shown him the holy city. But the angel resolutely rejects his worship, as he did after showing John the punishment of the great prostitute (19:10). The reason is as before: "I am a fellow servant with you and with your brothers the prophets"; but this time he adds a new group: and "all who keep the words of this book." This makes all who obey the words of John into servants of God. This is not to say that there is no difference in rank among the servants. We are not apostles, nor prophets, and certainly not angels.

Unlike Daniel, who had to seal his book and keep the

contents a secret (Dan. 12:4), because the future was still distant (Dan. 8:26), John is told not to seal his prophetic book because (and here he refers back to the beginning, 1:3) the time is near.

It will not be long now. The end is at the door. Therefore the distinction between Christians and non-Christians must become clearer. Wrongdoers are called upon to become even worse; the filthy are called upon to make themselves even filthier. But the righteous must offer a sharper profile of their lives. The saintly must be saintlier still. Something like this was already said in Daniel's prophecies (Dan. 12:10). History is about to climax. People are for or against. Light or darkness. White or black. Let there be no neutrality, no fog, no twilight condition. The "golden mean"—not to be too righteous or too wicked—is not for John.

Christ himself confirms that the return is near: I am coming soon (3:11; 22:7); I have my reward with me (Isa. 40:10), and everyone will be paid what he or she deserves (2:23; 11:18). The great day of reckoning has arrived. Justice will take its course. Christ is like God: the Alpha and the Omega (of God, 1:8; 21:6; of Christ, 1:17; 2:8).

John has heard the voice of Christ. His statements of congratulation and excommunication sound like echoes. They are happy who have washed their robes (cf. 7:14). They cleanse themselves in order that they may eat from the tree of life in the holy city. But dogs (Matt. 7:6; Phil. 3:2) and all sorts of lawbreakers must remain outside the gates (21:27). Their place is in hell (21:8).

John received God's revelation through Christ by way of an angel (1:1-2). Christ gives the assurance that this is indeed the case and adds that this revelation is meant for the churches. The servants of God may not keep for themselves disclosures concerning the end. In what Christ gave John to see and to hear he had in mind especially the churches.

Jesus repeats the words with which one of the elders comforted John when he wept because the scroll was sealed with seven seals: I am the Root of David (5:5). He is the Messiah as Isaiah prophesied (11:1). And the Morning Star, the symbol of royal sovereignty (2:28), is not only the reward of the person who wins, but especially the mark of him who has overcome as the Lion of the tribe of Judah (5:5), who overcame the ten kings as the Lamb (17:14), and who is seated as conqueror with the Father on his throne (3:21).

The Spirit and the Bride respond also to the assured promise of Jesus: I am coming soon (22:12). Here the Bride is the church, which is invited to the wedding feast of the Lamb (19:7-9). The same metaphor of the Bride, the wife of the Lamb, was used earlier for the New Jerusalem (21:2, 9). The Spirit prays for the coming of Jesus; and the church prays this prayer after him: "Come!" It is just one word, but that word includes everything that can be asked for. The other extreme is the "many words" (Matt. 6:7) used by pagans to put pressure on God. The persecuted church is like a ship in a storm. The telegraph operator signals just three letters, S.O.S., as a distress signal. When this passage about the Spirit and the church praying "Come!" is read in the churches, then everyone who hears it must take up the prayer: "Come!"

In this connection John reminds the reader of what God has said: To him who is thirsty I will give to drink without cost from the spring of the water of life (21:6). Then Isaiah's words are fulfilled: Come, all you who are thirsty, come to the waters; accept the water of life free to whoever wants it badly! (Isa. 55:1).

At the end of his book John appends a cursing colophon against falsifiers. This is not an uncommon practice. Although Paul dictated his Letter to the Galatians, he added the statement, "See with what large letters I am writing to you with my own hand" (6:11), as proof of its genuineness. Further, in his Letter to the Thessalonians, Paul warned them not to become unsettled or alarmed by a letter supposedly from him (2 Thess. 2:2). In Revelation, then, John adjures the copyists not to add to or subtract from his book. Since the art of printing had not yet been discovered, reproducing a given piece of writing was done by hand by copyists. Accidental mistakes could be corrected, but intentional changes in the text inspired by evil motives somehow had to be prevented. The method of deterrence was to direct a heavy anathema at possible falsifiers.

John's terminology is derived from Deuteronomy: "Do not add to what I command you and do not subtract from it" (Deut. 4:2, NIV; cf. 12:32). The hardened sinner who fancies himself secure from the imprecations addressed to those who trample on the commands of God gets to hear that all the curses written in the book will fall on him (Deut. 29:19-20). John lets the statement cut two ways: if anyone adds anything, God will add to him the plagues of Revelation; if anyone takes away from the book, God will take him away from his city.

The most awful punishment, therefore, hangs over the heads of the falsifiers. Did the threat help? It is hard to tell: even without magical formulas the text of the Old and New Testaments has come down to us with remarkable accuracy.

Revelation is not prophecy issuing from the will of man. John is the mouthpiece of Christ, the real author. This is all the more reason not to alter anything in the book. That author, Christ, for the third time in the conclusion offers the assurance: "I am coming soon" (22:7, 12, 20). To this the church responds with "Amen" and prays "Come, Lord Jesus." In Aramaic the prayer reads "marana tha." *Marana tha*, sometimes confused with *anathema* (both words appear in 1 Cor. 16:22), is a prayer that Jesus may come soon.

The beginning and end of Revelation correspond. The book, like a letter, begins with a greeting: "Grace and peace to you" (1:4), and ends with a benediction: the grace of the Lord Jesus be with all God's people. We opt for the (optative) form of a wish or prayer here. Because in the Greek the verb is missing, others prefer to use the indicative: the Lord is with you. The argument used in that case is that the officebearer does not utter wishes but assurances. In that light it is remarkable that the high priestly benediction of Aaron and his sons offers no firm assurance, but is an express wish (Num. 6:22-27).

So the last word of the last book of the Bible is a blessing. It is a blessing for the church, also for the church of today, if it understands and takes to heart the prophetic words of the Revelation of John.

CONCLUSION

In Revelation both the reader of its words and those who hear and take them to heart are pronounced blessed (1:3). It makes liturgical sense, therefore, to conclude the reading of Scripture in a church service with the words of Jesus: "Blessed . . . are those who hear the word of God and keep it" (Luke 11:28).

Hearing and keeping the words of God is not at all easy without accompanying explanation—a statement that applies especially to a book like Revelation. I hope that this volume has shed some light on material that is often hard to understand. A few questions remain, however, and we shall now consider them separately.

THE VERDICT ON THE JEWS

That verdict is extraordinarily sharp. Jews may say they are Jews but that is not true; they are lying, and therefore are a synagogue of Satan (2:9; 3:9). When the beast from the underworld kills the two witnesses, Moses and Elijah, the Jews celebrate, give gifts to each other, and leave the bodies on the street unburied. Jerusalem is called Sodom and equated with Egypt, Israel's archenemy (11:7-10), and it's inhabitants are as hardened as Pharaoh once was. Jerusalem is also called "the great city" (11:8; 16:19), which is definitely no compliment, for it is also an epithet applied to Rome (17:18; 18:10, 16, 18, 19, 21) and "Babylon the great," the archetype of prostitutes and perversities (17:5). In this regard there is in Revelation a parallel with the Gospel of John, where Jesus says of the Jews that their father is not Abraham but the devil, the arch-liar and murderer (John 8:44).

Can we simply appropriate this harsh judgment? It is understandable that in the heat of conflict people respond to each other in that fashion. Jews spread slanderous stories about Christians and falsely accused them, which often resulted in the Roman government imprisoning members of the church (2:9-10). But after the smoke of battle has cleared we may not continue to hold ourselves in such a negative posture. After all that Christians and pagans have done to Jews a certain amount of modesty is in order. Nor must we forget that the Scriptures say other things about Israel as well—see Romans 9–11, for example.

"SPATTERED WITH BLOOD"

To see God as the great Treader of the winepress is disagreeable to us (14:19). Isaiah pictures God as the field commander who tramples nations and whose garments are bloodstained (63:2, 5). What can we do with horses that wade up to their bridles in a river of blood 180 miles long (14:20)? This sounds almost sadistic. Before World War II we used to marginalize the psalms of vengeance (Ps. 137!). But during and after that war we who lived in Western Europe learned to understand those psalms better. For the rest, Marcion's heresy, which separates the God of the New Testament as the God of love from the God of the Old Testament as the God of vengeance, still plays tricks with us. This contrast, of course, is false. The God of vengeance is "merciful and gracious, slow to anger and abounding in steadfast love," a core statement that occurs seven times in the Old Testament (Exod. 34:6; Neh. 9:17; Pss. 86:15; 103:8; 145:8; Joel 2:13; Jonah 4:2). And the God of the New Testament is at the same time the God of judgment, and that not only in the Book of Revelation. Anyone who believes he or she will have an opportunity to gloat over the pain of others in the fires of hell simply does not know the Bible. Punishment takes place in the presence of the holy angels and the Lamb (14:10), and not before our eyes.

We certainly cannot delete judgment from the gospel. The loving Father is at the same time the righteous Judge; the reverse is true as well. The question is whether we can accept responsibility for the way images are used in Scripture. Father, Judge, King, Lord, Shepherd, Warrior—these are images. There is no other way for us to speak about God except in anthropomorphic images. We need to realize deeply, however, that God is God and man is man. Are there no bounds to be observed in the use of imagery? May we picture God as a blood-spattered field commander? And God's cavalry in a river of blood? Is this how one learns to know God? Or, in fact, man? Dare we picture Christ, the Rider on a white horse, as one who rules the nations with an iron rod (19:15; 2:27; 12:5) and dashes them to pieces like pottery? And can we use these images in a day when the just-war concept is no longer defensible and when the concept of a holy war only serves as a smokescreen to cover a fanatic religious nationalism? When a given image is no longer useful, we must drop it, however "biblical" that image may be.

THE CUBE

An important theme in Revelation is the depiction of future glory. The world of our present experience is the starting point and forms a contrast: no more hunger or thirst, no sunstroke or killing heat, no more tears (7:16-17) and no more death, no cries of fear and no more sorrow (21:4). The question is, must we understand the positive description of the heavenly Jerusalem as a precise report? The picture is that of a cube-shaped city, with a wall 144 cubits high, twelve gates made of pearl and streets of gold (21:9-21). Or is that simply a way of expressing perfection and unsurpassable beauty? That, in my opinion, is the case. We draw from the material at our disposal and note the precise point of comparison. If we fail to do that we get stuck. The prophet Isaiah saw God on his heavenly throne and the train of his robe was draped over the temple in Jerusalem (Isa. 6:1). That robe is a royal mantle and aims to depict the kingship of God. But if one rigidly insists that therefore God must be wearing a coat, questions irrevocably arise: Is it that cold in heaven? Is God dependent on higher or lower temperatures? Etc., etc. . .

THE PLAN OF GOD

The apocalyptic writer assumes that God has a certain plan and that history therefore unfolds accordingly. With a term derived from the Book of Daniel that plan is called "the things that will happen in days to come," or "what will take place in the future" (Dan. 2:28, 29, 45), phrases that John takes over (Rev. 1:1, 19; 4:1; 22:6). That plan is secret, but God has shown it to his servants the prophets. It is their privilege to look at things behind the scenes.

It has become apparent that John's prophetic work is rooted in quotations from the prophetic books of the Old Testament. The Book of Daniel, especially chapters 7 and 12, is an important source of information (see Rev. 13 and 17). The material for the plagues that will come over the world (Rev. 8, 9, and 16) is derived from the ten plagues of Egypt. Jeremiah (chaps. 50 and 51) and Ezekiel (chaps. 27 and 28) provide a palette of colors for the depiction of the fall of Babylon. Chapters 38 and 39 of Ezekiel are in the background of the war waged under the generalship of Gog and Magog (20:7-10). The New Jerusalem as a city of light (21:22-27) is unthinkable apart from Isaiah 60, and the holy city is inconceivable as a medical center apart from Ezekiel 47:1-12.

Then what is the revelational core? Does it consist in the

way John combines texts from the Old Testament? Or in the poetic liberty he takes in that process? Or in the use that he makes of the data? We may not forget that the real revelation consists in the prediction of the fall of the mighty Roman empire. The emperor who has himself venerated as a god must expect judgment, as must the priest who enforces the emperor cult as state religion and everyone who gives to the emperor that which is due only to God. There is a future only for those Christians who do not participate in the deification of the emperor. Everyone who firmly refuses to take part in it will share in the victory of God and his Anointed. That is the message John conveys and transmits, and therein lies the prophetic character of his book. The visions are the wrapping material; the important thing is what they contain. Images serve the Word. And the Spirit uses images and words to proclaim the eternal gospel (14:6).

THE MILLENNIUM

The millennium constitutes a special problem. For various sects it is an article of faith, but the church does not quite know what to do with it. Still, the millennium is not as strange an issue as it seems at first sight. Its origin lies in the Jewish expectation that the coming of the Messiah and his kingdom precedes the coming of God's kingdom.

The messianic kingdom is referred to in a number of New Testament passages. Without any attempt to be exhaustive I shall just cite a few of the more important ones. The angel Gabriel promises Mary that her son will rule as king over the house of Jacob forever and that his kingship will have no end (Luke 1:32-33). The disciples will sit on thrones to judge the twelve tribes (Luke 22:29-30). In Jerusalem stand the thrones for judgment, the thrones of the house of David (Ps. 122:5). Before Pilate, Jesus affirms that his kingdom is not of this world (John 18:36). Jesus does not deny that he will restore the kingdom to Israel but declares that the date is set by the Father (Acts 1:6). In Paul's writings the messianic kingdom is manifestly an interregnum, a period-in-between. Christ is raised first; at his coming those who are Christ's will be raised next; then comes the end, when the Son will hand over the kingdom to the Father. But between his return and the end Christ will rule. He must rule as king until he has put all his enemies under his feet. The last enemy is death (1 Cor.

15:23-28). And so the millennium is a modification of the messianic kingdom.

There are any number of theologians who reject the notion of a millennium. Calvin does not have a good word to say for the Chiliasts who with much gusto and the pretext of truth appeal to Revelation. He classifies their doctrine, along with other errors, under the rubric of "ravings." "But let us pass over these triflers, lest, contrary to what we have previously said, we seem to judge their ravings worth refuting," he writes in his *Institutes* (III.xxv. 5, 6; McNeill, 2:996). The *Confessio Augustana*, the Lutheran Confession of 1530, rejects the doctrine of the millennium in Article 17, sub. 5, as Jewish notions (*judaicas opiniones*). A similar judgment is made in Article 11 of the Confession Helvetica Posterior, the Swiss Confession of 1566, where these ideas are dismissed as Jewish dreams (*judaica somnia*). According to the Anglican Articles of Faith from 1552, they are Jewish ravings (*judaica deliramenta*). The Belgic Confession and the Heidelberg Catechism are totally silent on the subject.

The rejection of the millennium is understandable as a reaction against the fanaticism of some of the Anabaptists. Luther wanted nothing to do with the fantastic ideas of Thomas Münzer. The kingdom of Zion at Münster under the leadership of Jan van Leiden (1534/35) could only arouse strong feelings of aversion. But this does not end the matter for us.

The church father Augustine believed that the 1000-year reign referred to the church. To this day that interpretation has exerted strong influence, be it with numerous variations. One can fix its starting point at the conversion of Emperor Constantine (323) and its conclusion at the French Revolution (1789). The 1000-year reign then coincides with the Corpus Christianum. Other interpreters see its beginning at the birth or the Ascension of Christ and its end at the Second Coming. Hugo de Groot believed "the beloved city" to refer to Constantinople and Gog and Magog to be the Turks. But in 1453 Constantinople was conquered by the Turks while according to John the assault on the camp of the saints would not be successful! Abraham Kuyper regarded Gog and Magog, numerous as the sand of the seashore, as the Yellow Danger, and believed that China and Japan would march against the European-American peoples (*Van de Voleinding*, IV:354ff.).

The time in which Satan is bound is often viewed as the

period during which the gospel will have its ultimate penetration of church, state, and society. It will be a time in which there will be no neutral state or nonconfessing church. Governments will acknowledge the authority of the Word of God. The state, though never totally free from demonic traits, will be truly just (K. H. Miskotte, *Hoofdsom der Historie*, p. 429). There will come a long and happy period in which the oppressed will rule and the suffering church of Christ will be publicly vindicated. A political and social order will prevail in which the rule of Christ will be as manifest as it is possible in a world from which sin, suffering, and death have not yet been banished. A restored Israel will be the center of the world (H. Berkhof, *The Meaning of History*, p. 157). Israel restored as the center of the world? This is decidedly not a conclusion one can draw from a careful reading of John's Apocalypse. In this book Israel as an entity is finished (see the section on John's sharp verdict on the Jews at the beginning of this Conclusion).

For John the millennium is the reward of the martyrs. He uses Jewish notions of the future but at the same time criticizes the Jews. The kingdom of the Messiah is not for Israel but for those Christians who have paid with their lives for their loyalty to Jesus Christ. They rise from the dead but do not have to appear before the judgment seat of God to be judged in accordance with their deeds. The martyrs are exempted. This is how John comforts the persecuted church, and calls on it to persevere in the faith. The 1000-year reign is still future. It belongs to the final phase of history. To John the end was very near (1:3; 22:10). Since that time nineteen centuries have run their course. The Roman empire no longer exists. The final attempt to eradicate the Christian church has not yet been made. Martyrdom has not yet been publicly honored. There is no self-evident reign of Christ on earth. Anyone who believes, however, that he can dismiss the millennium as a Jewish notion had better listen to the warning of H. Bietenhard: the result is that one also has to reject many other teachings of the New Testament, such as the division between a present and a future age or the resurrection from the dead (*Das tausendjährige Reich*, pp. 162-63). Those who subscribe to the aforementioned articles of the confessions, where the millennium is dismissed as a Jewish fable, had better take this warning to heart.

THE BROAD CURRENT OF HISTORY

History has taken a different course from that which John prophesied; it's current has changed its bedding. John latched on to the idea that the Parthians would ruin Rome (6:2; 16:12). But we also find in Revelation that rebellion from within would put an end to the empire (17:15-18), a notion that can be compared with the hope that a given people would rid themselves of a dictatorial regime by way of a revolution. But the core of the prophecy is the victory of God and the Lamb over Emperor Domitian. The Beast and the false prophet would be thrown into the fire of hell (19:19-21). The truth is that Rome was not swept from the face of the earth during the reign of Emperor Domitian. After him came emperors who persecuted Christians even more severely than he did. Then something happened that remained completely outside of John's field of vision. Emperor Constantine the Great favored the Christian church and Theodosius the Great made Christianity the state religion! The (Western) Roman empire succumbed to the migration of nations, and Rome, the eternal city, fell into the hands of the Visigoths in 410. But the reasons for the fall were other than the worship of the image of the Beast (13:11-18).

John was convinced that the end of the world was at the door and so the victory of God and the Lamb would soon be a fact. Therefore the days of Rome and its emperors were numbered. Domitian, together with his priests and his devotees, would only last a very short while and then it was all over with them. That is the logic of apocalyptic literature.

John could not know that the end was a long way off. This is a fact that Revelation has in common with the other books of the New Testament. The early church expected the Son of Man to appear before the disciples, bringing the message of the kingdom of heaven, had completed their tour through Palestine (Matt. 10:23). Some of those who witnessed Jesus' activities would still see the Son of Man come back with royal splendor in their lifetimes (Matt. 16:28). For those early Christians the last days had come (Acts 2:17). Paul expected still to experience the return of Christ in the course of his earthly career (1 Thess. 4:15), and that applied also to his contemporaries (1 Cor. 15:51). At a later time he took account of the possibility that he might die before that event (2 Tim. 4:6-8). To James the coming of the Lord was near (5:8); for

Peter the end of all things had come upon them (1 Pet. 4:7). When there is a delay, the scoffers express their skepticism; but believers counter with the argument that it is God's wish for them to come to repentance, and that God operates with a different concept of time than we do (2 Pet. 3:3-10).

The permanent relevance of John's Revelation lies in its prophetic critique of the state. Whereas Paul still called on Christians to obey the Roman government as God's servant (Rom. 13:1-7), John sees the Roman government as the devil's lackey and prohibits participation in the deification of the emperor (chap. 13). Paul made his appeal to the emperor as the supreme judicial authority (Acts 25:11-12, 21, 25; 26:32; 27:24; 28:19), but himself later died a martyr's death! For John the persecution of Christians is proof that the government has exceeded the boundaries of its authority. The emperor assumes the characteristics of Antiochus Epiphanes IV, who taunted God by blaspheming, by desecrating the temple, and by trampling the truth underfoot (Dan. 7:7, 20, 25; 8:12-13; 9:26-27; 11:31; 12:11). The emperor degenerates to the level of the fourth beast in the night visions of Daniel (chap. 7). History repeats itself and will repeat itself many times, until the court will sit for the last time, the final tyrant is destroyed, and the people of the saints of the Most High God will receive the kingdom on earth (Dan. 7:26-27).